I Must Go Down To The Sea Again

The Story of a Deep River Mariner

(An Account of Historical Fiction)

Frank Hanley Santoro

Copyright © 2024 by Frank Santoro

All rights reserved.

ISBN: 9798346276999

Cover and Interior by Dominick Bosco

The image on the cover is a painting of the clipper *Flying Cloud* by the artist Jack Spurling. It was taken from the Wikimedia Commons website and is in the public domain. It also appears as the frontispiece to Chapter Eight. Its provenance information is contained in the About The Images section of this book.

Contents

The Stone House	v
INTRODUCTION	xi
1. A TALE OF THE SEA	1
2. ORIGINS	7
3. THE LANDING	13
4. A WHALING VOYAGE	21
5. YALE	33
6. THE WEST INDIES SUGAR TRADE	39
7. SHIPBUILDING	49
8. CLIPPER SHIP DAYS	63
9. THE CIVIL WAR	93
10. QUEEN OF THE VALLEY	101
11. SLOWING DOWN	113
12. LOOKING BACK	123
Epilogue	127
Acknowledgments	133
About The Images	135
Index	147
Bibliography	157
Also by Frank Hanley Santoro	159
About the Author	161

The Stone House
Home of the Deep River Historical Society
Reproduced with permission of artist Lori Lenz

This book has been produced in cooperation with the Deep River Historical Society but, as the story of the main character is a work of fiction, it is not an officially published Society historical document. As stated more fully in the Introduction, historical fiction can play an important role in making history come alive.

To Jane and Chris

SEA FEVER

I must go down to the seas again, to the lonely sea and sky,
And all I ask is a tall ship and a star to steer her by;
And the wheel's kick and the wind's song and the white sails shaking,
And a grey mist on the sea's face, and a grey dawn breaking.

I must go down to the seas again, for the call of the running tide
Is a wild call and a clear call that may not be denied;
And all I ask is a windy day with the white clouds flying,
And the flung spray and the blown spume, and the sea-gulls crying.

I must go down to the seas again, to the vagrant gypsy life,
To the gull's way and the whale's way where the wind's like a whetted knife;
And all I ask is a merry yarn from a laughing fellow-rover,
And quiet sleep and a sweet dream when the long trick's over.

John Masefield (1878-1967)

INTRODUCTION

The main character in this book is a man we shall call Joshua Standish.

But Mr. Standish is not a real person. He is a composite character representing what I have imagined to be the life of a Nineteenth Century Deep River River sea captain.

Why — you might ask — would I choose such an odd way to tell this story? The Deep River Historical Society has records about many *real* sea captains. Why make up history when real history is available?

The answer is that this story becomes more alive when told as historical fiction. Historical fiction can transport us to another time. Some of the best stories of the Nineteenth Century have come from its historical fiction writers: Walter Scott, James Fenimore Cooper, Herman Melville, Charles Dickens, Victor Hugo, and Leo Tolstoy.

The factual record of the Deep River seafarers is filled with data about births, deaths, voyages, captains' houses, ship's names, and speed records. But it doesn't tell you much about what these men were really like: what they loved, what they hated, who and what they knew, what they read, how they behaved, what they believed, and what were the events that shaped their lives. I have tried to fill in some of these gaps — to make their story read like it was written yesterday. My goal is to put flesh on the bones of history by painting a contemporary living portrait of these men and their times.

The story of Joshua Standish is obviously fictional. His adventures on a whaler, as a West India trader, a shipbuilder, a clipper captain, an officer in the Civil War, and the master of a coasting schooner are not historical fact. In some cases I have embellished his role. For example, in Chapter Eight I have made him the Captain of the clipper ship *Lord of the Isles* when the real captains were Peter Paxton and W. Jamieson. His role in the Civil War is exaggerated. But these adventures are representative of the activities of his real contemporaries.

With respect to everything *other* than the personal story of Joshua, I have tried to be accurate with history. This history includes the great events on the world stage such as the American Civil War, the California Gold Rush, the Opium Wars in China, and the Industrial Revolution. These events which had an effect on the imagined life of my Mr. Standish had a real effect on the actual Deep River seafarers who he represents. The fictional life of my Mr. Standish is intended to be a mirror of the history of the Nineteenth Century.

I have also tried to be accurate with sourcing. For

example, the story of the whaling voyage of my fictional Mr. Standish is based on the actual log of the same trip. The voyage carrying Captain Mather's younger brother Frank on the *Nightingale* from New York to Melbourne, Australia is based on Frank's published article. The subsequent voyage of the *Nightingale* from New York to Melbourne is based on an abstract of the log of that voyage.

The information about broader historical events is based on generally available information on the web or in libraries. Where the history is less complete, I have sometimes resorted to educated speculation. For example, I found a gap in the history of exactly how elephant ivory tusks made it from Zanzibar in Africa to the Landing in Deep River. I knew that it required ocean going ships which I assumed to be clippers at least until the steamers took over. I knew that American tariffs (the major source of federal income at that time) were high after the Civil War so I assumed that the ships would need to sail to the larger ports which had customs houses. This led to the further assumption that coastal sailing vessels would be needed to ferry the tusks to the Landing before the train service took over. In any event, I did not think it unreasonable that a blue water captain desiring to slow down would find the coastal trade attractive.

In the case of the known maritime adventures of Deep River seafarers other than Joshua, I have adopted the literary device of making them the stories he heard while on home leave.

It is important to note, however, that my retelling of

history is the work of an amateur. I have not consulted original sources with the rigor of a professional historian. I have not answered every question. I have not excluded all historical implausibilities. For a thorough recounting of the maritime history of the Nineteenth Century, one needs to look elsewhere. My limited goal is simply to tell a story about Deep River sailors.

In particular, I have employed a "Forrest Gump" quality to the life of my imagined Mr. Standish — the placement of him at an improbably high and diverse number of the major maritime events of the Nineteenth Century. I do not know if there was a real Deep River sailor for every single one of Joshua's adventures (although I think it likely). My main purpose was to illustrate the widespread impact of historical events on Deep River mariners as a group.

I have chosen to tell the story as a first person account — a common device for seafaring stories of the time ("Call me Ishmael"). This means the selection of a specific period of time for Mr. Standish's life (1810-1890). This time period captures the sweep of history from the aftermath of one revolution to the beginning of another (the Independence to the Industrial). Moving Mr. Standish around from one job to another also tends to exclude events before and after his tenure. This is especially true of the great clipper ship races which occurred after he left that trade for the American Civil War. It means the exclusion of events affecting Deep River mariners after his death in 1890. For these post 1890 events, I have used the Epilogue.

The seafaring story of Deep River is not unlike that of other towns such as Essex, Chester, or Haddam. With minor modifications, their mariners experienced the same adventures as my Mr. Standish. It is remarkable that such small river towns would have produced so many blue water sailors traveling around the world.

Lastly, I recognize that my choice of images to illustrate the text has been able to draw upon modern sources of reproduction that would have been unavailable to the autobiographical Mr. Standish. In choosing the images, I have relied on captions and artistic renderings evocative of the subject matter rather than literal representations of places, people, or situations. The full provenance of the images is explained in a section at the end of the book entitled About the Images.

If all else fails, my goal is to tell a good yarn. And there is nothing like a yarn of the sea. I have crossed the Atlantic six times by sea including once sailing through a hurricane (Cleo 9/4/64). Ever since I was a child, I have been fascinated by stories of seafarers.

One of the most magnificent structures built by man is the Nineteenth Century sailing vessel known as the clipper ship. The fact that some of the skippers of these ships came from Deep River should be a source of great pride for the Town.

The title is taken from the first line of *Sea Fever*, the immortal poem of John Masefield, the Poet Laureate of England from 1930 to 1967.

With the above as an introduction, I now introduce you to a man we shall call Captain Joshua Standish of Deep River, Connecticut born in the year of our Lord 1810.

Telling Tales of the Sea

Chapter 1

A Tale of the Sea

My name is Joshua Standish. I am from Deep River, Connecticut.

Throughout the course of my life, I have kept a log, a series of journal entries about my life as a mariner. In the sunset of my life, I have set them into a story. This is my tale of the sea.

I was born at home on Kirtland Street on Friday, June 15, 1810. My father's name was Elias and my mother's name was Martha. I have a younger brother Robert and a younger sister Gertrude.

I had a happy childhood growing up in the Deep River village of Saybrook. But from an early age, I was drawn to the lure of the sea.

In my late teens, I shipped out on the *Loper*, a whaling vessel out of Nantucket. We rounded Cape Horn and spent about a year and a half hunting whales in the South Pacific. I served as a deckhand during the voyage. The voyage was successful and my lay was tidy enough. But the ship's master was demanding and I was tired. I swore off whaling for the rest of my life.

After a few months at home, my mother pushed me to go to college so that I could become a minister. I spent a year at Yale and learned a lot. But I became impatient and yearned to return to the sea.

Back in the village, it was natural to be attracted to the Caribbean sugar trade. For six years, I shipped out on sailing vessels carrying the products of New England forests, farms, and industries to the Caribbean Islands and returning to Northern ports with sugar and rum. I worked my way up and eventually became captain of my own ship. But in 1834 at my age of 24, England freed the slaves of its Caribbean sugar plantations and the trade rapidly declined. I found myself back in Deep River without a job.

In the intervening years, the shipbuilding industry along the river was prospering and my father's connections soon landed me in a job in Essex. After a short time around 1836, Thomas Denison took over the Southworth yard in Deep River and I joined him and his son Eli for about a decade in a long and successful run of building blue water sailers. These included the schooners *Splendid*, *St. Deny's*, and *Deep River*, and the sloop *Forest*.

My shipbuilding days allowed me to go home every night and enjoy a domestic life. I married Sarah Waterhouse, the daughter of a Deep River merchant. We built our own home on Kirtland Street and had two children, Emma and Tad.

But the lure of the sea was never far away. As I reached

my 30's, it was becoming clear that a great new development was occurring in the seafaring trade: the rise of the clipper ships. Great fortunes be made in the clipper trade. And there could be no greater satisfaction for a seafaring man to skipper these magnificent vessels. I was hooked.

I sailed on three clippers during the next ten years of my life. The first was the *Sea Witch* out of New York first for China and then for San Francisco during the gold rush. In 1852, I started hearing about Sam Mather of Deep River. He had become a celebrity in the clipper trade when, in command of the *Nightingale*, he had made it from London to Java in the fastest time ever made. He then won a race with the *Challenger* from Shanghai to London. I asked to join his crew and we made four trips together to China and Australia. When Sam left the *Nightingale*, I left with him and secured a job which I loved — the Master of the British clipper *Lord of the Isles*. We made six trips from London to China. In one, we won a race with the clipper *Maury*. My clipper ship days were the peak of my career. I treasure not only my seafaring experience but the many friendships I acquired in foreign ports.

As the 1850's drew to a close, the clouds of civil war were gathering over America. Shortly after Lincoln was elected and the South fired on Fort Sumpter, I joined the Navy was was commissioned as a lieutenant. During the early years of the war, I served in the sailing ship *St. Lawrence* as part of the Atlantic Blockading Squadron. I was witness to the clash between the ironclads *Monitor* and *Virginia (Merrimac)* at the Battle of Hampton Roads in 1862. Because of my familiarity with foreign ports, I was reassigned to the *USS Kearsarge* which patrolled European waters. In 1864, I took part in the naval engagement with the Confederate ship *Alabama* off the coast of Cherbourg, France. When the war was over, I returned to Deep River and at the ripe age of 55 decided that it was time to stay closer to home.

Back home, the village was acquiring the title of Queen of the Valley because of the prosperity of its industries. This is especially true of the ivory industry. George Read had opened his new factory in 1851 and the Pratt Brothers had opened another one in 1856. Large quantities of elephant ivory tusks were being shipped from Africa to American ports and there was a need to ferry them up to the town landing. This was a perfect job for me. From 1865 to 1880, I was master of coasting vessels filled with ivory. But the railroads and the steamships were ascendant. The days of sail were coming to a close. It was time for an old sailor to retire.

But old sailors never retire. They just fade away. I joined the board of a local bank and did a little farming in Winthrop. Sarah and I visited our children who had moved to Boston. And I began to write this story. The chapters that follow describe my journey of life in greater detail. I am a plain spoken man and do not have the polish of the writers of my generation. But I hope you enjoy this story. It is a story of my times.

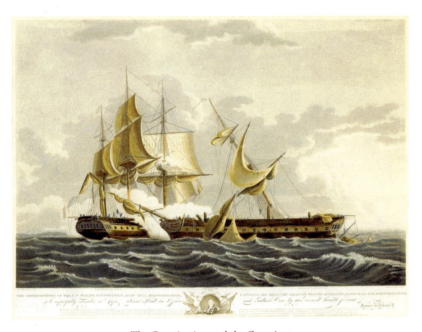

The Constitution and the Guerriere

Chapter 2
Origins

Family legend tells that I am a descendant of Myles Standish who came over on the Mayflower from England to Plymouth, Massachusetts. Myles' descendants drifted to Hartford with Thomas Hooker and then to the Saybrook Colony at the mouth of the Great River. Deep River is part of Saybrook.

My parents lived in interesting times. My father Elias was a shipbuilder. He fought with General Israel Putnam at the Battle of Bunker Hill. He obeyed Putnam's order not to fire until "you could see the whites of their eyes." He helped Jedediah Pratt of the Deep River village with the Colonial soldiers and aided in the provisioning of the brig *Martial* by which Nathan Post of the village attacked British shipping.

In the aftermath of the Revolution, New England became a stronghold of the Federalist Party. Unhappiness grew with the policies of the Jeffersonians — especially the

Embargo of 1807 which forbid foreign trade and idled many New England ships. The War of 1812 was unpopular in New England for the same reason. We even thought of signing a separate peace treaty with England. The war's effects on shipbuilding and trade had an adverse effect on our family's finances.

The War of 1812 was important here but for non-Americans it was considered a backwater to the Napoleonic wars in Europe. It was in 1812 that Napoleon crossed the Niemen and marched his troops into Russia. The Battle of Waterloo was fought only months after we signed the peace treaty with England. The British were impressing our seamen because they needed crews for the Royal Navy.

Despite their displeasure with the war of 1812, my parents were pleased with the victory of General Andrew Jackson at the Battle of New Orleans. Communications being what they were at the time, they did not learn until later that this victory actually occurred after the peace treaty had been signed with England.

My father had a love/hate relationship with the Royal Navy, then the most powerful military force in the world. He had been enthralled with its exploits in the Napoleonic wars and particularly with the tactic of "crossing the T" which had proved so successful for Lord Nelson at Trafalgar. But he was outraged at the British impressment of American seamen and the blockade of coastal ports. He was pleased with the victory of the *Constitution* ("*Old Ironsides*") over the *Guerriere*. He was angry when he heard of the British raid on Essex in the War of 1812. He was too late to attack the escaping British Marines but he did help in the rebuilding of the town.

My father briefly provided financial support to a privateer which had a letter of marque to attack British shipping. Unfortunately, the privateer was not very successful and he never saw any prize money.

Both parents regularly read the Connecticut Courant which was brought by courier from Hartford every week. It was one source of knowledge of the outside world. Another source was word of mouth which made its way through the network of seamen.

My parents were proud of their new country. They followed the Courant's reports of the Declaration of Independence and the Constitutional Convention. My parents were Federalists until the party faded away at the end of the second decade. They were unhappy when James Madison was elected president in 1809. My father voted for all eight of the first Connecticut governors (all Federalists) until 1817 when he voted for Oliver Wolcott, Jr., a Democratic-Republican. They idolized Stephen Decatur for his suppression of the Barbary Pirates. They loved Lafayette and were appalled at what was going on in Paris. My parents knew the difference between the American and French revolutions.

Shipbuilding was becoming important on the river. My father went into the business with Nathan and Job Southworth at the foot of Kirtland Street. His specialty was ship design. He helped to build the brig *Rowena* and the sloops *Wealthy* and *Alpha*. He was successful and was able to earn enough money to give our family a comfortable home. He was proud when his friend Joseph Post became master of the *Laquira*. Sailing was still king in my father's day but glimmers of change were on the horizon. He told me later that he had a sense of foreboding when he saw the first steamboat go up the river to Hartford in 1815.

My father helped in the affairs of the town. This included being a mentor to young men such as George Read, Joseph Post, and Sam Mather who were later to become famous. He was always lending a helping hand to his friends and neighbors.

My mother Martha was educated for women of her generation and instilled in me a great love for books and reading. She would borrow books from the traveling four town library and buy whatever books she could that were brought in by the seamen. Her favorites were the books brought from the London publishers. She was the first person in the village to acquire a copy of the new Dictionary by Noah Webster up in West Hartford.

Both parents rarely went to Saybrook Town and were pleased that the sand bar at the mouth of the river prevented the growth of a large city. At a time when some of the younger generation were attracted to Boston or New York, they were happy to be living in a small town.

Comings and Goings at the Landing

Chapter 3

THE LANDING

If I had to summarize my youth in three words, it would be the Landing, the Landing, and the Landing.

As I grew up in the second decade of this century, a widely heard phrase was the "Era of Good Feeling." It was meant by its proponents to convey an atmosphere of increasing confidence by Americans in their new country in the wake of the War of 1812. Whatever its political meaning, it is not a bad description of my life growing up in Deep River.

I was small when I was very young but as I entered the teen years, I grew to be tall and lanky. I had brownish hair and a fair skin made brown by my time in the sun. I was known as quiet but friendly and eager to learn new things and make friends. I got along well with my parents and my younger brother and sister. My father was stern, demanding, and rational. My mother was intuitive. My brother's personality was like mine. My sister was more rebellious and mischievous.

Our family finances were tight through the War of 1812 but began to improve thereafter. But we were no different from anyone else in town and never felt poor. I would earn small change from doing errands for the yard workers. This experience taught me the value of money, a value which helped me a lot in my later career on the sea.

As with most of our neighbors, our whole family were members of the Congregational Church. At first we had to attend meetings in other towns but switched to the one in town when it was built. In its first years, our minister was Orson Spencer who was an educated and tolerant man. Our church going habits inculcated a sense of honesty and moral righteousness. We obeyed the Ten Commandments. We enjoyed the services. We had many friends in the parish.

Our house on Kirtland Street had been built before we lived there. It was a standard New England farmhouse design. The Greek Revival style which became so popular later had not yet come to the neighborhood. The house was big enough for me and my sister to have our own bedroom. For me, the main attraction of the house was the fact that it was a short walk to the river landing. It was bustling at the yard on the landing but it was quiet up the street.

There was spotty formal schooling when I was young. There was a district schoolhouse on Kirtland Street with a rotating cast of teachers. It was enough for me to learn basic English, arithmetic, and reading. Most of my education was at the hands of my mother. We always had a few books around the house. This is true despite the fact that the reading of novels was discouraged by the town's puritan attitudes. My favorites were *Ivanhoe* and *Rob Roy* by Walter Scott, *The Swiss Family Robinson* by Johan David Wyes, *Rip Van Winkle* by Washington Irving, and *The Last of the Mohicans* by James Fenimore Cooper. My father would also bring home copies of the Connecticut Courant which he got in the village. My parents followed political matters but I did not care about that at all. Much of my education about the world was from the gossip of the seamen down at the yard. The piano craze had not yet taken place in the village and most of the music we knew came from the sea chanteys of the sailors.

The town of my fondly remembered youth was a pastoral reverie — a classic New England scene. As I grew out of childhood, I would seek the advice of my elders. Many were captains of the sea. Their stories left me wide eyed with wonder.

One day, I ran into Capitan Obediah Smith along the river. He was sitting down looking happy. I stood by his side.

"Sir", I said "I am no longer a child. I love it here in the village. But I don't know about the world. Every time, I see a boat go down the river, I want to go along with it. What is like down there? What is there to see?"

"Oh the places you can go" he replied. "There is a whole world to see. There is a world of adventure. Saybrook is down at the mouth. It is nice. It is where our ancestors first came from. It is off where we fought the British. You can go to New London. You can go to Hartford. But the world is getting smaller. If you really want a life, you should go to sea. You can go to London. You can go to China. The world is open to you. Yes, my son, you should go to the sea."

That was the beginning of my wanderlust.

My Son, You Should Go To The Sea

The village was compact and you could get anywhere by walking. The population was growing and there were many children my age. Most of them were children of farmers or seafarers. I was able to form friendships with many boys who later became sea captains like myself. Among my friends from Kirtland Street were John Saunders and Bill Palmer. Fun times involved fishing, imagine games, skating, culling on the ice, digging clams, and participating in spelling competitions. Playing cards and dancing were discouraged. When the Green store and Post Office opened in 1827, that became a favorite place to hang out. Our favorite imagine games involved soldiers, seafarers, and stories of the frontiersmen. As I grew into teenage years, I began to notice the girls in town. I had several girlfriends at the beginning but my first love was Mary Tyler from Winthrop.

But above all else, the major influence of my growing years was the lure of the sea that I picked up from the comings and goings at the Landing. I went there at every free moment. It was an exciting world where much was going on. I learned of Captain Nathaniel Palmer of Stonington who had discovered Antartica. I learned of the Monroe Doctrine. I learned of the wreck of the ship *Essex* by a whale in the South Pacific, a story that was later to inspire the novel of *Moby Dick* by Mr. Melville.

It was not hard to find stories of the sea close to home. This was especially true of the Post family — Deep River's dynasty of the oceans. When Connecticut was an English colony, David Post, Jr. commanded locally built vessels in the coasting trade. His son Joseph Post (1789-1878) was around town when I was growing up. He sailed on many ships and became master of the *Laguira* of New York when I was four. In 1825 when I was fifteen, he pioneered the New York-Mobile packet ship line which became known as the E.D. Hurlbut & Company. He retired to Essex in 1836.

Steamboats were starting go up and down the river. The paddlewheel steamer *Oliver Ellsworth* made regular stops at the Landing and I heard many stories from the crew and the passengers. We respected the crews of the steamers for their ability to handle the dangerous machinery but we never considered them seamen. We never thought that they would one day overtake sail.

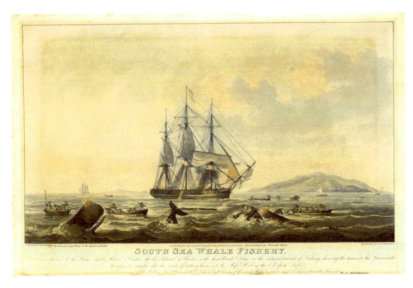

South Seas Whaling

Chapter 4

A WHALING VOYAGE

As I reached the age of seventeen, my happy domesticity began to turn to a curiosity about the world and a search for adventure. In my imagination, there could be no better way to sate this thirst was a whaling voyage to the far side of the world.

My parents and my girl friend were not happy at this prospect but they did not stand in my way. One day in the spring of 1827, I went to New London hoping for a spot on a whaler. As it turned out, there were no ships leaving New London when I got there. But a sailor told me that Nantucket was busier, that he was leaving for there the next day, and suggested I come along.

Nantucket was a dizzying beehive of activity. Whaling had been prospering there for a long time although its glory days were still to come. The harbor was filled with ships. Rare was the day when a whaler was not leaving or returning.

The economics of whaling were harsh for the novices such as myself. According to custom, whaling voyages were underwritten by a consortium of investors consisting of everyone from bankers, former captains, as well as widows' and orphans' funds. Ships were in constant need of crews and it was not hard to find a spot on board — no experience required. Everyone realized that voyages were long, hard, and dangerous. Often they lasted years at sea. Luck played a role in determining whether a ship returned full or empty. At the end of the voyage, the proceeds from the sale of cargo were divided between the ship owners and the crew. Each crew member was reimbursed according to his "lay"— a tiny percentage for the ordinary hands. The primary product from the voyage was whale oil stored in wooden barrels and used for illumination and lubrication. Other products were spermaceti, baleen, and ambergris. The crews were racially mixed and it was not hard to find a ship's complement consisting of white men from New England, Indians from the forests, and black men from the Caribbean.

After walking the docks for a few days and checking out the taverns, I signed onto the crew of the *James Loper* bound for the South Pacific and owned by the firm of L&J Starbuck and Company. The ship was named for a member of a famous whaling family from Long Island. The Master was Obed Starbuck of Nantucket. The Mates were Ned Palmer, William Griswold, and Tonto Walker, a Narragansett Indian. The ship was a three masted square rigger typical of the Nantucket whalers of the time. It carried a 22 man crew consisting of the captain, the three mates, a carpenter, a cook, four harpooners, and twelve deck hands who doubled as rowers when the boats were lowered to go after the whales. Of the twelve deck hands, five were black men from the West Indies.

On the evening of Tuesday, June 22, 1827 at 6 PM and with good winds at her back, the ship ghosted out of Nantucket Harbor and into the Atlantic. Before long we were out of sight of land.

This was the first time I had been to sea. As I look back on it many years later, I am reminded of my feelings by the recently published words of Alfred Lord Tennyson.

Sunset and evening star
And one clear call for me!
And may there be no moaning of the bar,
When I put out to sea.

Twilight and evening bell,
And after that the dark!
And may there be no sadness of farewell,
When I embark.

I DID NOT HAVE the watch that night and went to sleep in the forecastle exhausted.

A strange emotion came over me the following morning. The adrenaline which had been powering me for the past few days had abated and I felt a strange sense of loneliness and trepidation. I missed my family and the comfortable familiarity of Deep River. I began to regret my desire for adventure. It was only when the routine of shipboard life came to dominate my conscious awakenings that this sense went away.

As we passed the time at sea, I came to have great respect for my shipmates. The captain is the absolute master who holds the power of life and death in his hands. Absolute obedience is expected. The worst thing a neglectful sailor can be called is a "soger." But I got along well with the Captain and the mates. I became especially friendly with two members of the crew most different from myself: Tonto of the Narragansetts and Jerome Powell, a black man from Barbados. The relations between the captain and the crew were good and there was never any need for flogging.

The *Loper* sailed in a generally southerly direction although its precise path was directed by the winds. The plan was to round Cape Horn and hunt for whales in the South Pacific.

Let no one say that a whaling voyage is a vacation. The life of a seaman on a sailing ship is hard. You need to get your sea legs. You need to deal with sea sickness. We were divided into four hour watches. When off watch we slept in the forecastle which was dark, dingy, and smelly. Our meals were salted beef with biscuit and on Sundays a substance of flour boiled with water and molasses known as "duff."

When on watch, we were kept busy at the endless tasks required to keep a ship going (swabbing the decks, rigging the head pump, and the endless tarring, greasing, and oiling that is part of keeping the ship in shape). Everything seemed to be wood held together by string that constantly needed fixing. There is rarely time for boredom. As Mr. Dana put it in his book about his years before the mast:

*"Six days shalt thou labour and do all thou art able;
And on the seventh, holystone the decks and scrape the cable."*

A sailing ship is a maze of shrouds, cable, line, knots, fittings, and ropes of all sizes and shapes. Woe betide the sailor who does not "know the ropes."

One of the customs of the sea is for ships to "speak" to each other as they meet and closely pass by. The captains of the two ships will address each other through speaking trumpets which amplify their voices. Typical exchanges include winds, news from shore, and favorable hunting grounds.

The *Loper* spoke to many ships along its way. The first was on June 26 when we spoke to the ship *Superior* from New Jersey under Captain Wright which was also headed for the South Pacific. Unlike some other whaling voyages, we never had a gam where two passing ships exchange crews for social visits.

On July 3, we approached the Azores in the Atlantic. We were unable to land a boat on the Island of Flores in the Western Azores but we did manage to do some trading with the shore.

For the next month and a half, we sailed southward. We

spotted several whales along the way but did not go after them. On August 14, we spotted the Island of Trinidad. The weather was generally good although we were now sailing into the southern winter and occasionally encountered squalls. On August 27, a squall stove in our bulwarks and carried away the mainsail.

We were sailing south on a trackless ocean. At times, it seemed quite lonely. But we always knew where we were. The captain used the sextant to take sightings by the angle between the horizon and the stars and employed published tables and other devices to plot our course. I expressed interest and he taught me the basics of navigation.

As September approached, we reached the most challenging part of the trip — the route around Cape Horn. On September 16, we spotted Tierra del Fuego. There are three ways around the tip of South America: the Straits of Magellan, the Beagle Channel, and Drake's Passage. The first two are narrow passages difficult to navigate. As with most ships, we took Drake's Passage through the open ocean south of Tierra del Fuego.

For the next month, we made our way around the Horn encountering gale force winds most of the way. I must confess that this experience left me terrified. This was not like the Connecticut River. I had never experienced such weather.

The gales of the Horn dramatize the dangers of a sailor's life. Imagine what we had to do to going aloft to set or furl the sails. First we climb up a narrowing triangular rope ladder formed by the ratlines stretched across the shrouds.

When we reach the first step of the mast, we then have to crawl over the futtock shrouds which literally means climbing upside down. We then have to lay out on the yard working the sail while holding on for dear life with only a rope for a footfall and our arms and hands on the yard.

The farthest out man has to use an additional foot rope known as a Flemish Horse. All this without a safety harness. All this while the ship is moving wildly. And all this in windy and freezing weather when the mast is swinging over the side of the ship more than a hundred feet up in the air. It is scarcely a wonder that men are lost overboard.

Aloft in a Gale

Despite these hazards, Captain Starbuck took it all in stride and guided our ship safely around Drake's passage and up the coast of Chile. Along the way, we encountered the ship *Almira* out of Edgartown and the ship *Sara* out of

Nantucket. By October 25, we lay abreast the city of Coquimbo on the coast of Chile.

It was in late October that we began the hunt for whales in earnest. We got our first two whales on October 31. It was an experience that left me breathless.

For the experienced crew, the hunt itself was routine and they never experienced any major problems. Upon spotting a whale, the lookout would cry "Thar she blows" and the four boats would be lowered and rowed toward the whale.

Each boat carried a crew of six: the captain or the mate in the stern, four rowers in the middle, and the harpooner in the bow. Upon approaching the whale the harpooner would launch the harpoon into the whale and the chase (the "Nantucket Sleigh Ride") would begin.

The whale would eventually tire and die. The carcass would then be towed to the side of the ship and the blubber removed with flensing knives and "tried" in the brick oven on board where it would be turned into oil which would be stored in barrels.

My job was to be a rower and help with the trying and the cleaning up of the decks. We had a device for shooting the harpoon but it often mis-functioned.

Harpooning the Whale

Over the next ten months, we cruised the South Pacific capturing and processing a remarkably large number of whales. Some days would go by with no whales. On these days, a great boredom would set in. But on other days there would be a great many of whales. The highest number we caught in one day was eleven which we got on June 21, July 18, and July 28, 1828. By my count we got a total of 124 whales over this period and came up with 2140 barrels of oil, a very successful voyage.

Our landfalls were few and far between. In December over the Christmas period in 1827, we anchored for a few weeks near Tomba Village in the New Georgia Islands, part of the Solomons chain. In May and July 1828, we did some trading at the Hope Island Atoll in Kiribati in the Gilbert Island Group. In June 1828, we did some trading at Clark's Island in the Coral Sea between Australia and Papua New

Guinea. On September 13, 1828, we spotted New Zealand and came to anchor for a few weeks in the Bay of Islands in New Zealand before heading back north to home.

Despite the vastness of the Pacific Ocean, it was not unusual to come across other whaling ships from New England. Among the ships we saw or spoke were the *Pacific* of New Bedford, the *Plough Bay* of Nantucket, the *Phoebe* of New Bedford, the *Swift* of New Bedford, the *Chase* of Nantucket, the *Sophia* and *Connecticut* of New London, and the *Emirs* of Edgartown.

Yankee Whalers in the Ocean

Tragedy struck home on the way back. On October 17, 1828 our chief mate was lost overboard in a heavy sea and never seen again.

On the way back, we continued to see our fellow

whalers. We spoke the ship *Peruvian Mary* out of Nantucket and the schooner *Minerva* from Newburyport. By January 4, 1829, we were in the Gulf Stream. On January 10, 1829, we dropped anchor in Edgartown on Martha's Vineyard.

Our voyage was over. We were away for almost nineteen months, a fairly short voyage by whaling standards. We collected 2140 barrels of whale oil, a successful catch. Apart from the loss of a mate, our voyage was deemed a success.

After saying farewell, collecting my lay, and checking out my gear, I headed back to Deep River. I felt a bond with my crewmen and some of them remained friends for many years. But I cannot say that I was anxious for another whaling voyage. I needed time to recover. I did not like being away from land for so long. For the time being, I was glad to be home and took some time in deciding what to do next.

Yale College

Chapter 5

YALE

After I came home from Nantucket, I spent a few weeks doing very little. It was wintertime and there was not much to occupy my time. My pre-Nantucket girl friend had married someone else. I was content to be lazy. I figured that soon enough fate would present itself.

One day I was awakened from my doldrums by my mother who upbraided me for my inactivity. "You are now twenty years old. When are you going to make something of yourself," she said. As the confrontation proceeded, it became clear that her ambition for me was to become a minister, a respectable occupation in the community. If truth be told, she would also have preferred that I stick closer to home rather than roaming the world.

I had never thought much about the ministry. But it did not seem such a bad idea at the time. I was well read and studious. I liked to talk to people. I thought I had a moral code that would fit the role. And it seemed a far easier life than chasing whales in the oceans of the world.

In those days, there was only one place to go for a Connecticut man with ambitions in the Congregational Church: the College of Yale in New Haven. Yale was not far away. I could easily come home from time to time. And my family had the money to pay for the fees. When the autumn of 1830 came around, I found myself an entry level student at Yale bound for a life in the church.

Yale was already 129 years old by the time I arrived. It was named for Elihu Yale (1649-1721), an American born British merchant who had provided one of its original bequests. It occupied an impressive group of buildings in New Haven. Some of the students were from wealthier families than my own but I never felt alienated or patronized. I was older than most of the other students and my experience on a Nantucket whaler gave me a certain mystique. I did not have much by way of prior formal education but I never felt academically disadvantaged. The college had a strong identification with the Congregational Church. The Divinity School had not yet been founded but many of the students were bound for the ministry. Chapel attendance was compulsory. The president of Yale at the time I arrived was Jeremiah Day but the influence of its recent president Timothy Dwight was still very much in evidence. Among the professors were president Day, Benjamin Silliman, and James L. Kingsley.

At the time I arrived, the curriculum was heavily influenced by a document which had been introduced two years previously in 1828 by the Yale faculty entitled *Reports on the*

Course of Instruction. This report was a vigorous defense of the function of a classical education anchored on the study of Latin and Greek. It rejected the idea that a college education should ignore these "dead languages" and focus on vocational studies which were regarded as more relevant to a dynamic new nation. Many challenges to a classical education were being made including at the newly formed University of Virginia by Thomas Jefferson and at Harvard by Professor George Ticknor, a protege of Jefferson. The Yale Report was a major influence on American higher education.

The 1828 Report meant that my education at Yale was about as far removed from Nantucket whalers as one could imagine. My studies included Latin, Greek, Christian ethics, philosophy, history, arithmetic, and geometry. Whatever the merits of 1828 report as a matter of educational theory, I must acknowledge that I grew impatient with the drudgery of learning Latin and Greek. I liked the professors and my classmates but I had great difficulty with the relevance of much of my instruction.

My impatience with classical antiquity drove me to more interesting reading material which I found in abundance in the well stocked Yale library. My favorites were the the English romantic poets (Byron Shelly, and Keats), *The Pilot, A Tale of the Sea* by James Fenimore Cooper, *The Pirate* by Walter Scott, and *The Rime of the Ancient Mariner* by Samuel Taylor Coleridge.

You will no doubt take note that nautical works were among the books to which I was most attracted. As it happened, this was no coincidence. On a trip home to

Deep River one time in the spring of 1831, I chanced to come across Jerome Powell, my old friend from the *Loper* who was engaged in the seagoing trade to the Caribbean. Later that day in my family's house on Kirtland Street I had an epiphany. Yale was fine but the academic life and the ministry were not for me. The call of the sea beckoned again and could not be denied. Much to my parents' displeasure, I announced later that weekend that I planned to leave Yale after one year and return to a seagoing trade.

Brig Bound for Barbados

Chapter 6

THE WEST INDIES SUGAR TRADE

In my idle moments after Yale, I would often loiter around the Landing where I would pick up gossip. Invariably the subject of what I would do next came up. One day, John Carter, a friend, said "Why don't you try the sugar trade." This was not a total surprise. So I set out to learn what I could.

The West Indies trade had been going on for centuries. Originally pioneered by the Spanish and Portuguese, it had largely been taken over by the British and Americans in recent years. It was a major industry in New England.

New England farmers and craftsmen would bring their excess crops, animals, and other products to merchants who would in turn arrange with sea captains to carry it to islands in the Caribbean. Once in the Caribbean, the captains would use local merchants to trade it for the products of the sugar plantations.

Caribbean Sugar Plantation

The ships would bring the sugar (and sometimes molasses and rum) back to New England ports where it was much in demand. It was typical for a local ship to make several trips a year: normally once after the fall harvest and once again in the spring after the ice had thawed. The ships were typically two masted square sailed brigs built at local shipyards. The voyages often headed for the more southerly Caribbean ports such as Barbados and sailed back on the trade winds stopping as necessary in various islands along the way. The Caribbean islands selected for trading were largely at the discretion of the captains and the network of merchants along the way.

Shipping the Sugar

The economics of the trade were favorable. Merchants and sea captains could make a good profit if they were efficient. The trade was helpful to the Americans in the Revolution where Connecticut acquired the nickname "The Provision State" for its ability to supply Washington's Army. The trade suffered under Jefferson's embargo and the War of 1812 but resumed if not quite at the same level as before. The West Indies traders came from all across the East Coast of the United States but especially from New England.

The Connecticut River was prominent in the trade because it was easy for ships to sail near the source of the farmers' markets. The first West Indies trader from the Connecticut River was the ketch *Diligent* from Saybrook owned by Robert Lay of Potopaug (Essex) bound for

Barbados. For a time, the City of Middletown became quite rich from this trade.

This trade seemed a good fit for me. It would allow me to return to the sea but in trips that were short compared to years at sea in whaling ships. It would allow me to return home for stretches between trips. And it was not hard to find a place. There were many Deep River captains who could take me on.

It was thus in the year of 1831 that I signed on with Captain Shailer of Deep River to sail as First mate in the brig *Amity*. Our first trip began in May when we left Deep River to head up to Middletown where we picked up a cargo arranged by the merchant firm of Alsop and Company. The cargo consisted of 20 barrels of salted fish, a consignment of machetes and other tools used in the cane fields, 10 horses to power the sugar mills, 100 sheep, a load of of barrel staves, and 50 board feet of lumber. The trip south took about a month and was quite pleasant. The weather was fair most of the way and the company of the small crew of 10 was nice because it consisted of many friends from along the river. The handling of the ship was not difficult and the there was time on board for card games and my favorite pastime of reading books.

We pulled into Bridgetown Harbor in Barbados where we dealt with local merchants known to Captain Shailer. We were fortunate in being able to unload all of our cargo and pick up a load of sugar. I was able to go ashore for a few days and be a tourist. Barbados was a pleasant place at least in the well manicured British Colonial precincts. It was only later that I was to learn of the conditions on the sugar plantations. We still had some room in our hold and picked up a small additional load of sugar in Jamaica on the way back. We returned to Middletown and gave our sugar to the Alsops to sell. Then we sailed back to Deep River to take some time off. All in all, it was a very satisfying trip and my pay was fair. The only cloud was the gossip along the way that the trade was in decline. I was only later to learn why. We made a similar trip the following fall and my experience was largely the same.

As the year passed, my thoughts turned to running a ship of my own. It seemed an ambitious plan at first but I was able to pull it off. I had friendly relations among the local seafaring community and I was now regarded as a competent and honest sailor. I obtained a loan from some local merchants as well as my parents and recruited a crew. By now, I had become familiar with the merchants in Middletown: the Alsop and Watkinson families.

But it was necessary to have a connection with a merchant in the Caribbean. Here is where my whaling experience proved helpful. My friend Jerome Powell from the *Loper* was from Barbados. I wrote to him and learned that he had an uncle in Barbados named Elias Powell who was a prominent merchant in Bridgetown — one of the few merchants who was not white and British. After a series of exchanges of letters, I was able to connect with Mr. Powell. This allowed me to sail safe in the knowledge that I would have a ready buyer for my New England produce when I arrived.

For the next two and a half years, I happily engaged in the West Indies trade generally making two or three trips a year. I believed I was a competent captain. Many of my crewmen were my friends. On one trip, we took along the wife of one of my crew. It was unusual for a woman to be a crewman but she did an excellent job and I began to think women could even be better than men for certain roles. The trips were easy and the weather was fair. There were no wars involving America or the European powers and piracy on the sea had been largely eradicated by the patrolling warships of the United States, England, and France, Most of the time, our trips were between Middletown and Barbados. In Middletown, I continued to deal with the Alsop and Watkinson families. During this time, I became a close friend of Elias Powell in Bridgetown and enjoyed many days in trading and learning about the island. I found the British merchants correct and efficient but snobbish and patronizing. I preferred to deal with Elias.

On one trip, I had a little extra room in the hold and Elias suggested that I stop in Nevis on the way back. I was curious to see a mountainous island — a contrast from the flatness of Barbados. He told me that Nevis was attractive, that it was another British colony, that it also had sugar, and that he had a friend there who was an agent. He told me that Admiral Horatio Nelson had met and married Fannie Nisbet of the island when he was there in command of the HMS *Boreas*.

He also told me that Nevis was the birthplace of Alexander Hamilton. I knew that Hamilton had spent his early years as a clerk with the trading firm of Beekman and Cruger on St. Croix and had become an expert on the West

Indies sugar trade. It was that experience which had given him a hatred of slavery and had taught him the economics he later used to run the American Treasury.

I followed Elias's advice and fell in love with Nevis. It was everything he said it was. The island is small and is dominated by a mountain which is often obscured by clouds. The Spanish named it Nevis (snow in Spanish) because the mountaintop seemed always covered by white clouds. As with most other islands in the West Indies, it is covered by sugar plantations. It was also administered by a wealthy British gentility. From then on, it became one of my regular spots.

As I became accustomed to the West Indies trade, I came to a dawning awareness of slavery on the sugar plantations.

By the time of my voyages, most of the islands of the West Indies had become a monoculture of sugar production. This was especially true of the larger islands such as Barbados and Jamaica. Sugar was known as "White Gold" because of the enormous fortunes it generated. Many of the British plantation owners spent their time in high society in London and never visited the Caribbean plantations they owned. There was a powerful lobby in Parliament known as the London Society of West India Planters and Merchants which advocated for sugar and slavery. Many of the lobbyists were themselves members of Parliament. I had visions of them sipping cherry in their clubs and partying in Mayfair and Belgravia. This mass production of sugar was made possible by the labor of cutting the sugar cane in the fields.

Cutting the Cane

I asked Elias about it one day.

"You don't want to know" he said. "What do you mean?", I replied. "It is hard on the plantations. The ships bring over the slaves from Africa and they are sold to the planters who work them on the land. I don't know whether it was worse in Africa. But the planters are afraid of slave revolts. They don't want us to talk about it. I just try to keep my nose clean."

I was aware of slavery in the South but had never experienced it personally. I had stayed away from the maritime slave trading from Africa and looked down upon the captains who practiced it. I had always had abolitionist sentiments from my Congregationalist faith. I was aware that Mr. Garrison had started his abolitionist newspaper the *Liberator* in Boston and that Prudence Crandall had opened a school of young black women in Canterbury. Connecticut had abolished the slave trade in the aftermath of the Revolution. There were slaves in Connecticut in the early Nineteenth Century but none in Deep River that I knew of. I had enjoyed equal relations with black men from my experience on the *Loper*.

My awareness of slavery on the plantations never made me want to abandon my role in the trade. Perhaps it was willful ignorance. Perhaps it was the fact that my stops in the ports never involved visits to the cane fields. Maybe, I just wanted like Elias to "keep my nose clean."

In any event. the British were ahead of us Americans in getting rid of slavery. By the time of my voyages, the system of slave labor in the Caribbean was in decline. England had outlawed the slave trade in 1807 and the Royal Navy was beginning to enforce the prohibition. Abolitionist sentiment was growing in Parliament largely due to the efforts of William Wilberforce. In 1834 England freed all its slaves in the Caribbean. The plantations continued to operate but on a less profitable basis. Substitute sweetener products began to develop. The West Indies trade was already slowing and these developments pushed into terminal decline. I suppose it can be said that all this hurt my pocketbook but helped my conscience.

My days in the West Indies trade were over. It was once again time to try something new.

The Launch

Chapter 7

SHIPBUILDING

At the age of 25, I found myself out of trips to the West Indies and back in Deep River. I was forced to sell my share of my ship because I needed the money. I continued to live with my parents on Kirtland Street.

But times were good. We were still in the "Era of Good Feelings" and the ship building business was flourishing along the river. There were no places at Southworths' but, using my father's connections, I was able to get a job at the Denison yard in Essex. Basically I became a so-called "jack of all trades." It was depressing after being the master of my own ship. But it was a steady wage.

And then fortune intervened. In 1836, Thomas Denison moved his business from Essex to Deep River and took over the yard that had been run by the Southworths. Thomas and later his son Eli operated a successful ship building business at the Landing for 35 years. My career was set — at least for the time being.

The Denison Shipyard

In my new position with Tom Denison, I was still a jack of all trades but my position was elevated to a supervisory one. My seagoing experience was regarded as a qualification for ship design. I was able to make design changes to the hull and the sail configuration based on the projections as to the wind conditions in which the ship would likely be traveling. Once the design was set, I then supervised the process in which lumber would be assembled.

There were many yards along the Connecticut River building wooden sailing ships in those days. In the Essex yards alone in the 106 years from 1776 to 1882, there were no fewer than the phenomenal number of 423 ships built.

Perhaps the most famous ship built in Essex was the first one: the 300 ton warship *Oliver Cromwell* built by Uriah and John Hayden. The ship was commissioned by the General Assembly for the Connecticut Navy for use in the Revolutionary War and was launched on June 13, 1776. It captured nine British ships during its service including the *Admiral Keppel* off the Island of St. Kitts in the Caribbean which was carrying the British diplomat Henry Shirley who was en route to Kingston, Jamaica. It was itself captured after a sea battle off Sandy Hook by the British in July 1779 and renamed the *HMS Restoration.*

I was always surprised that the builders in Essex had chosen to give the name of Oliver Cromwell to a ship built to fight the British. Perhaps it was to poke the nose of the Royal Navy.

The Oliver Cromwell

In Deep River, the yard at the Landing was dominated by two families: The Southworths and the Denisons. Job

Southworth started in 1793 by building the 40 ton sloop *Hannah*. Between then and 1836, he built ten more (in one case added by Charles Tiley). Thomas Denison took over in 1836 and between then and several decades later he and later his son Eli (occasionally aided by others) built 53 more ships concluding with the small sloop *Acme*. The Denison yard built several steam vessels but could never sustain a profitable business doing so and went out of business near the end of the century.

Even a small yard involved a complex manufacturing process. Materials had to be sourced. Customers had to be obtained and contracts signed. Designs had to be adapted to intended use. Workers had to be recruited, trained, and paid. Specialized tools were required. Winches and cranes had to be used for heavy objects. Woods had to be selected with care and applied with preservatives. Caulking, copper, glues, and nails were needed. Sailcloth was obviously necessary. The launching always involved a small ceremony. The Denison yard had the capability to launch a ship sideways — a technique which sometimes proved more feasible.

The construction process involved the laying out of the blocks, the setting of the keel, the forming and assembly of the ribs, and the final construction of the decking and the masts. Special attention had to be paid to the construction of the bow and the stern and the raking of the masts because it was these features which gave the ship its special profile.

The first ship we built at Denison's was the schooner *Splendid* in 1836. It was a two masted vessel 67 feet in length and weighing 87 tons. It was built for Epaphroditus Bates with whom I spent many hours discussing his requirements. The owners were Bates himself and a consortium of ten other local seamen and businessmen.

We built two more ships in 1836: the *Emily* and the *Pompino*. Until the time I left in 1845, we built many more ships including the *St. Deny's* and *Forrest* in 1838, and the sloop *Deep River* in 1839.

The Denison yard was slowed by a financial panic in 1837 but it affected the factories in town more than us and the town in general was not as affected as businesses and banks in the cities.

In 1839, an incident occurred which caused the scent of the sea to enter my nostrils and stimulate my conscience. Word along the docks reached us that a Coast Guard cutter had intercepted a Spanish slaver and towed it to port in New London. The name of the ship was the *Amistad*. It seems that the slaves had staged a mutiny, killed the Spanish crew, and were trying to sail back to Africa when they were intercepted. At first the authorities had trouble figuring out what had happened but then miraculously they found a sailor on the docks who could speak Mende, the language of the Africans.

The Amistad

What followed was a lengthy legal controversy over what to do with the ship and the would-be slaves. Many Connecticut abolitionists took up the cause of the slaves and the case eventually ended up in the Supreme Court of the United States with a decision in favor of the Africans giving them their freedom. My abolitionist sentiments had been increasing and I went myself to watch one of the legal hearings in New Haven. I was pleased at the final result.

In the meantime, my work at the Landing allowed me to spend all of my time in the village and I began to experience a normal domestic life.

One morning as I was leaving the service at the new Congregational Church, I spotted a young woman who attracted my attention and who I had never seen before. I asked a nearby friend who she was. He told me that she was Sarah Waterhouse — a daughter of one of the proprietors of the new Green Store. I asked if he could make an introduction which he did at the next Sunday service.

Sarah and I began to see each other a lot. She was beautiful and smart and she had many of the same values as I did. I was proud to be with her. She was always in my thoughts. I could barely think of anything else. It was the springtime of my life and I was in love.

We courted for about 6 months when I asked her father for permission to ask her to marry me. Both he and she said yes and we were married at the church on Sunday, May 10, 1840.

Now that I was a married man with a good job, it was time to think about building my own house. There was never much doubt that it should be on Kirtland Street. I bought an empty lot a few houses up from my parents and Sarah and I started to think about what we wanted.

At that time, there was a new architectural style coming into fashion. It was known as Green Revival. The style involved a traditional wood built house with an entrance at the gable side in the front. It acquired the Greek name because the frontal decoration vaguely resembled that of an ancient Greek temple. In the interior, the house would have a parlor in the front and the dining and kitchen area in the rear. Just inside the front door, there would be a staircase upstairs where there would be several bedrooms. Unlike the older houses of the time, it would not have a fireplace because stoves were coming into fashion for heat.

A Greek Revival House

OUR HOUSE FOLLOWED this traditional pattern. I built it myself with the help of carpenters from the yard. When it was finished, it was the source of great pride and satisfaction on the part of both Sarah and I.

Shortly after moving in, our son Tad was born. He weighed seven pounds and was a happy and easy baby. Having a child to take care of was a transformative experience and it made me more risk averse than I had previously been. I could no longer think of myself quite as much as before and had to think of taking care of others. I still had ambitions of going to sea and I struggled with the idea that doing so would take me away from home. Two years later, our daughter Emma was born. She was a bit cranker as a baby but grew up to be mischievous as a young girl. Both children were a joy to have around the house.

While I was enjoying domesticity, others were making their mark on the sea. Hanson Arnold, a native of East Haddam, moved to Deep River and was a coasting captain and master of several Deep River built vessels. He was the father of Justus and Joseph — both mariners like their father.

Calvin Williams, a native of Essex, married Eunice Southworth of Deep River and was master of several vessels in the local and Texas trade. He built a beautiful stone house on Kirtland Street in 1826. He had two sons including Richard Calvin Williams who was five years younger than me and also also became a sea captain.

Life in town settled into a pleasant pattern. Joe Post retired as a captain and a year later his son Pritchard was born. The Post family would grow to be one of the most prominent seafaring families on the river. In 1837, Dr. Edwin Bidwell took over the medical practice of Dr. Rufus Baker. Stephen Jennings began to expand his manufacturing business. Unfortunately, a fire destroyed his new factory in 1837 and he had to start over. Through a mistake, the insurance had lapsed on the building a day before the fire. Cal Rogers' business making looking glasses and woodturning novelties was prospering. The ivory business was beginning — a business that would later grow into a major business of the country and a business that I would later join. Among its pioneers were George Read and the Pratt brothers. Stone quarry businesses were operating in several of the more easterly parts of town. For a while, it seemed like practically everybody in town was named Pratt, Jennings, Southworth, Post, Denison, or Watrous.

While my focus was mostly in the town during these years, I tried to keep up with the affairs of the state and the nation. The whaling industry was reaching its peak in nearby New London. In 1838, a railroad was built between New Haven and Hartford. When I heard this news, I began to wonder whether railroads would eventually take over from ships. Martin Van Buren was elected president in 1836 to be later followed by Benjamin Harrison and John Tyler. I had become a member of the Whig Party and thus supported Harrison and Tyler. A popular political song of the time was "Tippecanoe and Tyler Too". It went as follows:

For Tippecanoe and Tyler too
For Tippecanoe and Tyler too
And with them we'll beat little Van, Van, Van
Van is a used up man
And with them we'll beat little Van

I hummed it often as I worked around the yard.

I continued to have a love of books and tried to keep up with what was available, My favorite was a new book by Richard Henry Dana called *Two Years Before the Mast*, a seafaring book which reminded me of my *Loper* days. I was also becoming a fan of the newly emerging writers of New England such as Henry Wadsworth Longfellow, Ralph

Waldo Emerson, and Edgar Allen Poe. Although his works were harder to obtain, I was also hearing about a new author in England called Charles Dickens.

The news of affairs in the world reached us by sea. In 1837, Victoria became the new queen in England. We also began to hear of a famine in Ireland as ships arrived in New York carrying families from that country. I never knew anyone on the crews of the ships carrying these passengers.

What interested me most, however, was the information I was beginning to hear about new advances in design for square rigged ships built primarily for speed and known as clippers. The name most often associated with these designs was Donald McKay — a man born in Nova Scotia of Scottish parents and who had been involved in the design of ships in New York, Maine, and Massachusetts. In 1845, McKay opened his own firm in East Boston. Curiosity got the best of me and I went up to see it and had the good fortune of spending a few hours with Donald and hearing about his vision for this new means of transportation.

Sarah seemed to share my interest in clippers but after I came back from seeing McKay, she started becoming unusually quiet. I asked "What is wrong." At first, she said "nothing." But it continued and when I persisted she finally said one day "I am afraid. If you go on clippers, you will never be home. You will be far away around world and on dangerous passages. What about me? What about the children?"

I couldn't deny that this was a problem. Was I just

thinking about myself? Would it be better to just stay home, build ships at the yard, and leave the sailing to others? We talked about it for many weeks. Sarah eventually came to a form of acceptance. Maybe it was because so many other wives in town were having the same experience. Maybe it was because this was a way to make a family fortune and live contentedly in retirement when the voyages were over. Maybe it was because of the village culture. I promised not to continually stay at sea and to come home between trips. By the time I was ready to go, we were happy with the plan.

By this time, I had spent about ten years at the Denison yard in Deep River and I was getting restless. I was inspired by the experience of meeting McKay and seeing his operation. It was time for me to make another move.

The Flying Cloud

Chapter 8

CLIPPER SHIP DAYS

Of all the masterpieces of man, there are few more wondrous than a clipper ship.

A clipper ship is a large wooden sailing vessel. It mounts three stepped masts (fore, main, and mizzen) each of which carries various tiers of descending square sails known from top to bottom as skysails, royals, topgallants, upper topsails, lower topsails, and main sails. It also has three sets of fore and aft mounted sails: jibs on the bowsprit, staysails between the masts, and a spanker at the stern. It has a streamlined hull with a tapered bow and stern. It is built primarily for speed. A fully rigged clipper in a fair wind is a sight to behold. In the middle of the Nineteenth Century, clippers were the greyhounds of the sea.

In the 1840's, the Americans were the pioneers of the world of the clippers. Of the clipper designers, Donald McKay was the most prominent in Boston and John W.

Griffiths was the most prominent in New York. The British soon followed in the next decade. By the middle of the century, there were many clippers in the world. Among the most famous were the *Flying Cloud*, the *Cutty Sark*, and the *Thermopylae*. For a captain of the sea, the command of a clipper was the peak of the profession.

I should say parenthetically that a clipper as I use the term was different from an earlier form of sailing vessel known as a Baltimore clipper (a smaller fore and aft rigged vessel).

The original clippers were all wooden but later versions were known as composites because they had wooden hull planking on a steel frame. Clipper ships were typically built for shipping agents and for particular trades. Among the the most common of the trades were the tea trade from China and the Gold Rush trade to California and Australia. Speed was important for the tea trade because the first harvest of the tea was regarded as the best and there was some spoilage during the voyage so that the first arrival in America or England could command the highest prices.

The typical route for a tea clipper was round the world. A ship from London, New York, or other American ports would sail across the Atlantic, around the Cape of Good Hope, and across the Indian Ocean and then north to China. A common passage between the Indian Ocean and the South China Sea was the passage between the islands of Java and Sumatra past Angier Point — a marker well known to navigators. At various Chinese ports, they would trade their cargoes for tea, silks, porcelain, and other Oriental products. They would then sail for home by crossing the Pacific Ocean and rounding Cape Horn. The heaviness of the Chinese porcelain was considered useful ballast by the clipper captains.

This worldwide trade had cultural effects on New England beyond merely expanding the wallets of its captains and traders. Sailors returned from the Orient with porcelain and furniture which graced the homes of many prosperous families. To this day, "Chinoiserie" is considered a stylish form of home furnishing. The popularity of the pineapple on New England wallpaper is reputedly based on the exotic nature of the fruit when brought back home intact by fast sailing ships or as a sign of a welcome homecoming by a proud captain. Dinnerware from Canton or Nanking was admired for its blue hand painting and became so popular that the term "China" became generic to virtually all fine tableware.

International trade was dominated by many powerful merchant trading houses. Among the most well known were Howland & Aspinwall in New York and Russell & Company and Jardine Mathesen in China. Both were to play roles in my life.

Russell & Company was formed in 1824 in China by Samuel Russell who was born in Middletown, Connecticut and came to Canton in 1819 as a trader. By 1842, it was the largest American trading house in China dealing primarily in silk, tea, and opium. Russell had returned to Middletown when I had worked at the Denison yard and I had heard of his adventures and was always curious about such an interesting man living not so far away.

The Jardine firm was formed in 1832 by William

Jardine and James Mathesen, two Scottish Oriental traders. By the early 1840's Jardine had set up in Hong Kong and had ten clippers of its own sailing the world. Jardine Mathesen has since become legendary in Hong Kong history.

The Russell and Jardine firms operated together in a cooperative relationship. They frequently dealt with a Chinese man known as Howqua who was head of the Canton Cohong (Export Import firm) and was once thought of as the richest man in the world. The Western leaders of the China trade were known as the Tai Pans.

Howqua

The China trade was accelerated by acts of British imperialism known as the Opium Wars.

The early trade was mostly British but the American competition became so great that Parliament abolished the monopoly of the East India Company in order to open up the trade to other British merchants. The Qing (Manchu) dynasty in China was reluctant to trade with westerners who they regarded as inferior barbarians. Westerners who received an audience with the emperor were required to perform the "Kow-Tow" (a bow to the ground). The Chinese limited trading to the so-called "Thirteen Factories" in Canton and demanded payment in gold and silver. The British became tired of the drain on their cash reserves and sought to solve their balance of payments problem by trading with opium— a narcotic drug native to Turkey and grown in British Bengal.

The opium dens of China began to fill up. The Qing Emperor Daoguang became alarmed at the spreading addiction of his people and ordered the opium stocks destroyed without paying compensation. Tensions started rising.

An opium den

Daoguang Emperor

THE BRITISH MERCHANTS took umbrage at the destruction of their opium stocks. They took up the cry of "free trade" and complained to Parliament. Their pleas initially fell on deaf ears with the Duke of Wellington. The opium trade was controversial in England. William Gladstone, a prominent member of Parliament, called it "infamous and atrocious" and with respect to the opium wars said he felt "in dread of the judgments of God upon England for our national iniquity towards China."

But Lord Palmerston, (the then British Foreign Secretary) was of a different political party and a different view and it was he who was then in power. On a trip to London, William Jardine persuaded Palmerston to send a naval force to force the Chinese to open up their ports. This became known as the First Opium War (1839-1842). The Chinese were no match for the Royal Navy and Marines and the war ended with the Treaty of Nanking (1842) by which the Chinese opened up several treaty ports, allowed the opium trade, and ceded the island of Hong Kong to the British. Two years later, the United States obtained essentially the same concessions as the British by the Treaty of Wangxia (1844). The Second Opium War in 1856-1860 was a continuation of the first and resulted in the imposition of additional unequal treaties on the Chinese.

A Scene from the Opium Wars

These new arrangements facilitated the rise of the clipper tea trade.

That is where I came in.

I went up to Middletown where I had the privilege of meeting with Sam Russell and learning of the enormous potential of the China trade.

Sam was twenty one years older than me. He was an enormously successful and powerful man living in a grand house. I was a little nervous as I approached his door.

The Samuel Russell House

"Good morning, sir" I said "It is an honor to meet you." He could not have been more gracious and friendly. "Call me Sam" he said "I hear you are interested in the China trade. As it happens, that is something I know about."

He spent the next few hours telling me about the enormous financial opportunities of trading in China. He regaled me with stories of the Tai Pans, the compradors, and the inscrutable Chinese. We both realized that my interest was in sailing a ship rather than working in a trading house but that did not dim the ardor of his conversations. He admitted that life could be hard so far away from home but that the compensation was the financial reward. He promised to put in a good word on my behalf if needed. As we passed the time, I began to get the feeling that he missed the adventure of his days in China and was reliving it by talking about it to me.

I interviewed at Howland & Aspinwall in New York. This landed me a position as First Mate on the clipper *Sea Witch* on the tea trade to China. I was very proud of myself because the *Sea Witch* was one of the earliest American clippers and was considered the fastest ship in the world at the time.

The *Sea Witch* was designed by John W. Griffiths for Howland & Aspinwall and launched at the South & Dimon Yard in New York on December 8, 1846. It was designed to carry porcelain and tea. It was 192 feet long and weighed 908 tons. It carried five tiers of square sails on each of its three masts. The mainmast was 140 feet high. Its streamlined hull was a revolutionary design. It's record speed of 74 days from Hong Kong to New York is the fastest ever recorded for a monohull vessel.

The Sea Witch

I began my duties on the ship's maiden voyage under Captain Robert H. Waterman. Waterman was known as "Bully Bob" because of the relentless manner in which he pushed the crew. I found him to be harsh but I served a useful purpose in smoothing out his relations with the men. We left New York shortly before Christmas in December 1846 and made it to Hong Kong in 104 days.

This was the first time I had ever been to the Orient. I found it fascinating. I learned about the ancient civilization of China. I took as much time as I could to see the temples and the houses of worship that were so diffcrent from our own. I tried to meet the people but found this to be difficult because not many of them could speak English. I heard about the Chinese opium dens but never saw one. This was not a subject dwelt upon the American and British traders and it was only later that I fully realized what a scourge opium had been in Chinese society.

Sometimes, the clippers carried a supercargo — a man whose job was not to sail the ship but to look after the cargo on behalf of the owners and to do the trading at the ports. When we did not have a supercargo, one of my jobs as a First Mate was to help with the negotiation of the trading.

By the time I came to China, Sam Russell had returned to Middletown where he built his stunning Greek Revival mansion known as the Samuel Wadsworth Russell House. William Jardine had died several years before and James Mathesen had left the business for England where he became a member of Parliament. He also bought the entire Island of Lewis in the Outer Hebrides of Scotland where he built a castle near the town of Stornoway. When I arrived the Russell firm was in the hands of Robert and Paul Forbes and Warren Delano, Jr. and the Jardine firm was in the hands of David and Andrew Jardine. I was to negotiate with all of these gentlemen and began a friendship with them which continues to this day. I suspect that Yale helped with my social acceptance. Forbes and Delano certainly knew of it and the Jardines had heard of it from the missionaries.

After completing our business on the first voyage of the *Sea Witch*, we left from Whompoa Reach (the port of Canton) and on July 25, 1857 reached New York by way of Cape Horn after a voyage of 82 days. Our second voyage was a round trip on the same route at 104 days out and 77 days back. My third voyage under Captain Waterman was on a different route. In 1848, we sailed from New York to Valparaiso Chile by way of Cape Horn and then to Hong Kong and back to New York. In 1849, Captain George W. Fraser took over for Waterman and I made one more trip under Fraser to Hong Kong.

Meanwhile gold had been discovered in 1848 in California. This created a huge demand for passage from the East Coast to San Francisco. The travelers became known as the "Forty-Niners." Several shipping lines provided passage from the East Coast to Panama and Nicaragua and thence up to San Francisco. Many of these ships were steamers which were beginning to make their appearance on the world's oceans. But there remained a demand for fast passage by sailing ships around Cape Horn. Shipping companies advertised their service by "Sailing Cards" which were widely distributed along the docks of port cities such as Boston and New York.

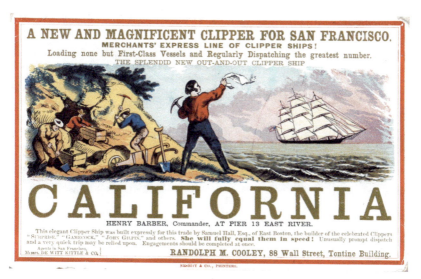

A sailing card

Howland & Aspinwall adjusted their business accordingly and for me, this meant a new route. Between 1850 and 1852, I made two passages on the *Sea Witch* around the Horn from New York to San Francisco. One of them involved a return trip by way of China.

San Francisco was a busy place when I first arrived. California had only recently become part of the United States under the Treaty of Guadalupe Hidalgo which had ended the Mexican American War. Not long before, San Francisco had been a sleepy settlement of only several hundred people. Like Hong Kong which it slightly resembled, it was becoming a boom town. By 1849, the population had swelled to 40,000. The harbor was crowded with ships bringing passengers seeking their fortune. It was sometimes hard to find a mooring.

San Francisco 1849

The city bore the marks of a boom town. The harbor was filled with rotting square riggers abandoned by their crews off to the gold fields. Social conditions were chaotic. Most of the population were rowdy young men spending their money on gambling and prostitution (the latter at an area called the Barbary Coast). The streets were paved with planks. Health conditions were terrible. There was a cholera epidemic in 1855. Chinese immigrants arrived to work in the gold fields. But the signs of growth were there. In 1853, an immigrant from Bavaria named Levi Strauss opened a dry goods store. Tycoons such as Mark Hopkins and Leland Stanford were getting their start. What I found most amusing was a hotel called the Niantic named after a whaleship built in Connecticut. I did not stay there — too noisy — I preferred the ship. All in all, I found San Francisco a most unpleasant place. I preferred Hong Kong.

The Niantic Hotel, San Francisco

I was able to make visits at home in Deep River during gaps in my travels around around the world. I was always euphoric when I arrived and morose when I left. Sarah was doing a wonderful job managing the household and taking part in the affairs of the village. The family was well provided for because my employers always sent my pay home. Tad and Emma were growing. When I came back in 1852, Tad was ten years old and Emma was eight.

When I was home in the village, people would ask about the art of sailing. They knew how small fore and aft rigged boats like sloops could sail against the wind but they also knew that square riggers worked differently. They marveled about how we could make it around the world. They asked how we could do it when the wind was not at our back.

This was a difficult explanation for something that was so second nature. It is obvious that no sailing vessel can travel directly against the wind and for all sailing ships there is a pie shaped wedge on the top of the compass against which it is impossible to move. But even for square riggers, it is possible to move forward by going sideways. I usually began my explanation by saying that square rigger sailing upwind involved a complex choreography of wind, wave, sail, and seafaring ingenuity.

The first way, of course, to avoid sailing against the wind is to find a route where the prevailing winds were at your back. Sailors had been doing the for centuries and we did this whenever we could. There were well established routes where these conditions prevailed. We would take advantage of the Tradewinds (East to West) or the Westerlies (West to East) and find the way to our destination even if it meant sailing indirectly. In ancient times, this was known as the Brouwer Route. We called it the Clipper Route.

But sometimes sailing against the wind became a necessity. We did this by turning the direction of the ship and moving forward in a zig zag series of motions known as tacking. Turning with the wind on the bow was known as coming about and turning with the wind on the stern was known as wearing ship (jibing in a sloop). Tacking in a square rigger is more difficult than in a fore and aft rigged ship like a schooner but it is not impossible.

We would make these turns by maneuvering the positions of the sails while making adjustments at the helm. Even square riggers have some fore and aft mounted sails: jibs on the bowsprit, staysails between the masts, and a spanker at the stern. And the square sails could be adjusted by changing the angle of the yards on the masts. Forward motion of the ship could be maintained by a proper balance between the wind pushing sideways and the inertia of a heeling hull moving straight. Forward motion could also be maintained by an aerodynamic principle discovered by the Swiss mathematician named Daniel Bernoulli by which air passing over a billowed surface like a sail creates a vacuum on the forward edge pulling the sail forward. Movements like this could create forward motion about 70 degrees off the wind and allow a ship to sail in an arc in all but 6 points to the compass or what would be between about 2:30 to 9:30 on a clock.

Needless to say, these motions demanded the highest standard of seamanship on the part of the captain and the crew. Listeners rarely failed to be impressed with learning about such skills and their respect for their neighbors who were seamen increased accordingly.

There were plenty of people to be impressed with. Home visits allowed me to catch up on what other Deep River seafarers were doing.

Hanson Arnold had two sons who both became mariners. Justice Arnold worked as a rigger and sailed for thirty years. He was master of the schooner *Gertrude* and the sloop *Luna*. His brother Joseph H. Arnold sailed as First Mate under his uncle Asahel Arnold on the clipper *Robert Center* and took over when Asahel died at sea. He later served as master of the *Ocean Belle* and later became chief inspector for the Sun Mutual Marine Insurance Company.

The Robert Center

The Saunders brothers both became sea captains. John N. Saunders served as master of the schooners *Splendid, John Q. Adams, Charter Oak, Charles Carrol,* and the steamer *Henry C. Beach* all built in Deep River at the Denison yard.

I was saddened to hear that Thomas Massie Collins, three years younger than me, died at age 32 of yellow fever while in command of the brig *Linden* out from Mobile bound for Newport.

Calvin Williams (he of the stone house) had a son Richard Calvin Williams, who was five years younger than me and also became a sea captain commanding several vessels. He had an interesting retirement. In his later years, he married an Italian Countess and moved to San Remo, Italy where he died in 1877.

The dangers of the seagoing trade were illustrated by the fate of Captain William B. Palmer III. A native of East Haddam, Palmer had married Charlotte Shipman of Chester and moved to a home on Kirtland Street near the Landing. In 1855, he set sail for New York as master of the *Eudora Emmagene* with a cargo of lumber. The ship was found sunk at at the western end of Long Island Sound. Eventually Palmer's remains were found and the ship's cook was found guilty of the murder and promptly hanged. Palmer's remains were brought back to Deep River and buried at the Fountain Hill Cemetery.

In 1852, I started hearing about the exploits of Samuel W. Mather — a fellow seafarer from Deep River. Sam was 14 years younger than me. I did not know him well but I remembered him from the village.

Samuel W. Mather

Sam had been placed in command of the clipper *Nightingale* with an intent by its owners to avenge a loss in a race with the British ship *Challenger* from London to Shanghai.

The Nightingale

The *Nightingale* was a 185 foot clipper launched in New Hampshire in 1851 and intended by its owners Sampson & Tappan of Boston for the China and Australia trade. It was named after Jenny Lind, a popular Swedish opera singer who was touring America at the time and known as the "Swedish Nightingale." Its first voyage was from Boston to Sydney.

In 1851, Sam was given command of the *Nightingale* with the encouragement of Commodore Robert B. Forbes, a prominent China trader.

The influence of Forbes showed the value of

networking among the China trader community. Forbes was born in 1804 in Boston and was a prominent China sea captain in his early career where he was involved in the ownership or construction of approximately seventy vessels. By the mid Nineteenth Century he was active in the Russell Trading firm in China where he amassed a great fortune. He later returned to Boston where he became a prominent citizen founding a retirement home for sailors and — like Sam Russell — building a Greek Revival Mansion. His recommendation of Sam Mather obviously carried great weight.

Sam's first voyage was from London to Shanghai. His time from London to Angier Point in Java on the way was the fastest time ever made. In the return trip to London, the *Nightingale* beat the *Challenger* back to London by more than a week. In the seafaring world, Mather had become a celebrity.

I wanted to join him. I was proud of the Deep River heritage.

Accordingly, I bade my leave from the *Sea Witch* and wrote to Sam to ask if I could join him. I mentioned the interview I had with Sam Russell in Middletown when I was still at the Denison yard. To my great delight, he said yes. From 1853 to 1856, we made four trips together from London and New York to China and Australia.

On one of the trips, we carried Sam's brother — a boy in his teens. The ship was chartered by the Australian Pioneer Line to carry cargo and passengers to Melbourne at the height of the Australian gold rush. We left New York Harbor on May 19, 1853. The plan was to reach

Melbourne and then sail to China to pick up tea and silk with return to London. We sailed on a new more southerly route with better winds. After sailing over twenty five thousand miles, we made land after 75 days and with mere minutes off the calculated arrival time. Our arrival in Melbourne was greeted with excitement and Sam was feted by the local dignitaries.

When we arrived, an unusual event occurred. Disappointed by the refusal to allow them release to the gold fields, the crew staged a mutiny and were imprisoned by the Australian police. When it was time to sail, Sam demanded his crew back and despite their sullen nature was able to make it to Hong Kong. From Hong Kong, we made a trip to Whompoa Reach and took a steamer side trip up to Canton. After carrying a cargo up to Shanghai, we sailed to London where the ship was sold.

Another example is the trip from New York to Melbourne, Australia in 1854. We had general cargo and 125 passengers and made the trip in 75 days. At noon on May 16, the steamer left us outside the bar in New York and we made for the sea under foggy weather. On June 20, we encountered strong winds and put up our topgallant sails for the first time. We encountered variable winds throughout June and July and made it to Hobson's Bay, Melbourne on August 2.

Sam Mather left the ship after the 1856 trip and I left with him. I am glad I left because the ship's history was not so illustrious in its later years. It was captured carrying slaves by the *USS Saratoga* in 1861 and turned into a naval vessel doing blockade duty during the Civil War. It also was used to lay cable in the Arctic. Eventually it was abandoned at sea en route from from Halifax to Liverpool.

Having served in lower offices in the clippers, I was now determined to be a captain myself. This was more difficult on the American ships because the owners had many able captains from which to choose. But the British were catching up in the clipper trade and Americans with China experience were a valuable commodity. After looking around a bit, I reached what I regard as the apex of my career — the Master of the British clipper *Lord of the Isles* bound for the China tea trade.

The Lord of the Isles

Lord of the Isles was one of the first British clippers. She was built in Greenock, Scotland in 1853. She was 210 feet and 770 tons. She was unusual in that her hull was built of iron — a rarity for clippers. She began service in 1853 with trips to Australia.

I joined her in China just in time for what turned out to

be her most famous voyage. A race was arranged between us and the American clipper *Maury* to see which ship could reach London first with a cargo of the year's new crop of tea. We left Foochow in northern China on June 10, 1856 bound for London with the *Maury* following closely behind. Remarkably and after a 127 day voyage over thousands of miles of ocean sailing, we both reached Gravesend on the Thames within ten minutes of each other. We had a better tugboat and ended up first at the dock.

My favorite port in China was Hong Kong — an ideal harbor. Hong Kong proper is an island which lies just south of a jagged protrusion from the southern Chinese mainland known as Kowloon. Off in the distance north of Kowloon is a mountainous area known as the New Territories. Hong Kong lies east of the estuary of the Pearl River which runs up to Canton. West of the Pearl is the Portuguese settlement of Macau.

Hong Kong itself is quite mountainous. The main settlement and harbor lies on the north of the island and the perimeter is lined with villages such as Aberdeen, Repulse Bay, and Causeway Bay. The highest point is known as the "Peak" and it is there that the Tai Pans have their mansions which afford a fantastic view and a more accommodating climate than the island's prevailing humidity. I have spent many a pleasant evening in the company of David Jardine on the Peak sitting in a rattan chair gazing on the busy harbor below and enjoying a proper English gin (Tanqueray not Gordon's).

When I arrived, Hong Kong was in the process of transition from a small fishing village into an international trading hub administered as a British Colony. At any given time, the harbor would be filled with western ships and Oriental crafts such as junks and sampans.

The highest offices were reserved for the British but the population was overwhelmingly Chinese. The British worked with cooperating local officials known as compradors. Increasing economic activity acted as a draw to the mainland Han Chinese many of whom felt oppressed by the Quing rulers who were themselves an alien race from Manchuria.

The Americans were represented by a consular official. Christian missionaries started arriving. Scotsmen Thomas Ash Lane and Ninian Crawford opened a store on the island and it soon grew into a retail emporium. As I look back on it after forty years, Lane and Crawford remind me of Levi Strauss. There was a fair amount of piracy because of the absence of the Royal Navy which was occupied on the other side of the world in the Crimean War. A condescending imperialist attitude prevailed among the British and there was discrimination against Chinese. British treatment of the Chinese was to foster a rising Chinese nationalism which began to find expression later in the century.

One of the customs of Hong Kong was for the Jardine militia to fire a gun salute to welcome the arrival of the Tai Pans by sea. After I left, I heard about an incident in which a British naval officer became annoyed by this practice because he believed that it was a prerogative reserved for government officials. As a punishment, the Jardines were ordered to fire the gun every day at noon in perpetuity. That practice endures to this day.

For the Tai Pans in Hong Kong, life was pleasant enough. It compensated for the hardships of being far away from home. Most lived in expansive houses surrounded by servants. Some brought their families. Others sought companionship and sexual relations with local concubines (concubinage was common in China). Social occasions were limited to fellow westerners. Delicacies were often imported from England. British customs and sports activities prevailed. For most Tai Pans, the goal was not to live forever in China but to make a fortune and retire home. I found it a pleasant place to visit but I would not have liked to live there.

Hong Kong, 1850

Between 1856 and 1859, we made five more trips to China. All were uneventful. After our return to London on March 14, 1860, I left the ship because of the war clouds gathering in America.

My leaving the ship was bittersweet because the years that followed saw some of the greatest events of the China trade. This is especially true of the Great Tea Races.

By this time in the century, England had become a nation of tea drinkers. The tea came from China. The task of getting the tea from China to London became a cultural event.

Because the first crop of tea commanded the highest prices, it became a competition to see who could get to London first. Clippers raced from the ports of China to the Thames. Newspapers followed closely. Bets were made in China and London. Sea captains became celebrities.

The most famous race was that of the *Ariel* and *Taeping* in 1866. After leaving on the same tide and sailing thousands of miles, they raced to the Thames within minutes of each other while breathless onlookers observed from along the shore.

The Ariel and the Taiping

Another famous race took place in 1872 between the *Cutty Sark* and the *Thermopylae*.

Alas, the glory days of the clippers were fading by the end of the decade. Steamers were taking over. The *Agamemnon* was the first steamer to make it all the way from China. The Suez Canal opened in 1869.

But it was time for me to leave all this behind for the next chapter in my life.

The Kearsarge and the Alabama (Edouard Manet)

Chapter 9

THE CIVIL WAR

I HAVE ALWAYS BEEN AN ABOLITIONIST. I have hated slavery, more so when I read Ms. Beecher Stowe's book about *Uncle Tom's Cabin*. I acquired a respect for black people from my days on the *Loper*. When I commanded the *Lord of the Isles*, I gained a respect for the British and was proud of the fact that they had outlawed slavery before we did. I went to see Abraham Lincoln when he spoke in Connecticut. I could not vote for him because I was at sea but I was happy when he was elected.

When the Southerners fired on Fort Sumpter and began to secede, I knew we were in for trouble. There was never any question in my mind about joining the war effort. The Union Navy needed experienced men and I fit the bill. The higher commands went to the professional Navy men but there was plenty of room for us from the commercial services. Before long, I found myself with a commission as a lieutenant and a new mission in life.

Shortly after the beginning of the war, Lincoln ordered a naval blockade of the Confederacy. General Winfield Scott came up with a plan to patrol the Atlantic Coast, the Gulf of Mexico, and the Mississippi River. It was called the Anaconda Plan. The idea was to strangle the South's economy. The blockade lasted many years. It was not very effective in the beginning but became more so as the years went by.

The Confederacy perfected the art of blockade running by using fast steamers often built and manned by British crews and using neutral ports in the Caribbean. The typical blockade run would carry out Southern cotton and other raw materials for transshipment to England's mills and bring in arms and ammunition that the South could not manufacture on its own.

The Union did not have many ships in the beginning but that was changed by a massive shipbuilding program. Steam propulsion had begun to replace sail. Most of the blockade ships were steamers but there was still a fair number of sailing ships and also many of hybrid power. Blockade duty was considered a boring job. It was fairly safe because Southern blockade runners were rarely armed. The blockade was porous especially in the beginning of the war. Most of the blockade runners were able to evade the Union Navy. Legal issues arose when ships flying neutral flags were stopped. Because they were small and built for speed, the runners could not carry much cotton and by the end of the war, the textile industry in England had suffered. The Confederacy had hoped that England

and France would come in on their side but both countries stayed neutral.

The Union blockade forces were divided between the Atlantic and the Gulf. The Atlantic force became divided between North and South Atlantic squadrons. I was assigned to the North Atlantic Squadron which patrolled from the Potomac River to Cape Fear in North Carolina. My squadron commander was Louis Goldsborough until he was replaced by Samuel Phillips Lee.

Most of my time was spent on the frigate *St. Lawrence*, a three masted sailing ship which resembled the clippers I knew. The *St. Lawrence* was launched in 1848 and was employed in various duties in Europe, the Pacific, and Brazil until it was added to the Atlantic squadron in 1861.

We patrolled up and down the coast catching two blockade runners, the schooner *Petrel* of Charleston and the British schooner *Jenny Lee* carrying rice and tobacco from Georgia.

The Sinking of the Petrel

In early 1862, we joined the Union fleet blocking Hampton Roads, the gateway to Norfolk and Richmond. We were there to watch the battle of the ironclads. On March 8, 1862, the Confederate ironclad ship *Virginia* (formerly the *Merrimac*) came out to attack the Union squadron and did a great deal of damage to our wooden ships on the first day of the battle. We joined the battle but ran aground. We exchanged fire with the *Virginia* but our shells bounced harmlessly off its iron plating. A shot from the *Virginia* penetrated our starboard quarter and did considerable damage causing us to withdraw. The following day, the Union ironclad *Monitor* arrived on station and battled it out inconclusively with the *Virginia*. The shells of two ironclads bounced harmlessly off each other. The battle of the ironclads was an inflection point in naval warfare. The age of wooden ships of war was coming to an end.

The Monitor and the Merrimac

In April 1862, I received devastating news. Sam Mather had been killed in action.

Sam began Civil War service in the gunboat *Quaker City*. In 1861, he was transferred to the armed steamer *Henry Andrew* and ordered to patrol the coast of Georgia and Florida. On March 22, 1862, Sam and a small party came under fire in an expedition to the shore near the Mosquito Inlet in Florida. Nine men including Sam were killed and several others wounded.

I had not kept up with Sam since the *Nightingale* but I was not surprised that he had joined the fight. He was that kind of man. He was the first man commissioned from the commercial service by by Gideon Welles, the Secretary of the Navy. When his body was brought back to Deep River and buried at the Fountain Hill Cemetery, I took leave to come back and wish him farewell. Secretary Welles said that he had no superior in his rank.

I was demoralized from Sam's death and asked for a change of assignment. In recognition of my familiarity with foreign waters, I received orders to join the *Kearsarge*, a hybrid steam sloop of war which was preparing to hunt the Confederate raider *Alabama*.

The *Alabama* had become notorious in the Union Navy. She had been built near Liverpool and launched by the English over a Union diplomatic protest. Over more than a year, she had made seven expeditionary raids over the oceans of the world capturing or burning sixty-five Union merchant ships.

In June 11, 1864, the *Alabama* put in for repairs at the port of Cherbourg in France. Three days later, the

Kearsarge arrived and took up station outside the harbor. On June 19, the *Alabama* came out into international waters and the two ships fought it out within sight of onlookers from the shore who included the painter Eduoard Manet who painted a picture of the scene. Our gunnery was superior and the *Alabama* was reduced to a sinking wreck. We rescued most of the survivors but the captain escaped on a British yacht.

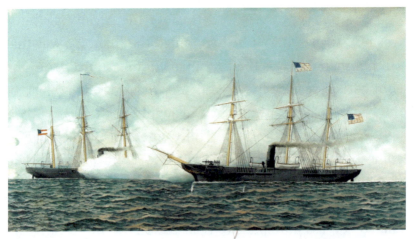

The Battle of Cherbourg

An interesting legal development occurred about five years after the war. The United States brought a monetary claim against England contending that it violated neutrality by allowing ships (mainly the *Alabama*) to be constructed and launched knowing that they would be used in hostile actions against the Union. By the Treaty of Washington in 1871, the two countries agreed to an international tribunal to meet in Geneva and adjudicate the claim. The final award was $15 million to the United

States and almost $2 million to England. This process is considered to be a major step in the development of international law and the role of the City of Geneva in international affairs.

After the Battle of Cherbourg, we did additional patrolling in European and Caribbean waters and were decommissioned in 1866 at the end of the war.

The Civil War was over. I was now 55 years old. It was time to return home.

A Coasting Schooner

Chapter 10

Queen of the Valley

THE SPAN OF MY LIFE EXTENDED FROM ONE REVOLUTION TO another. When I was born, the American Revolution was a recent memory. By the time I left the Civil War at age 55, the Industrial Revolution was in full swing.

For the first time in history, machines were doing the work that had been previously done by man. The power of a man's muscle rose a hundredfold. New inventions proliferated. Human slavery became less important. New use was found for the world's waters. Gravity and sloping topography turned water into hydropower. Wood and coal turned water into steam. Man could make things faster and in greater numbers. Populations increased. Cities grew. A new era of economic progress and prosperity had been unleashed.

The industrial revolution had a great effect on the shipbuilding and seafaring trade.

The Denison yard was still building sailing ships after

the Civil War. It built the *Vail* and four other schooners and two sloops in 1866 but it closed in 1870 when it tried to build steamships without success.

Ships powered by steam were taking the place of ships powered by sails. I must confess that this left me with a bittersweet taste. For me there was no peer to the majesty of a vessel under full sail. But I could not help but acknowledge that steam made it possible to carry goods from one place to another without relying on the winds.

The Vail under Construction with the Wahginnicut Hotel in the Foreground and Eustacia Island in the Background

The Industrial Revolution began in Britain, a country with a large population, an empire, plentiful supplies of coal, and a developed legal system. The British invented the steam engine and various machines for the manufacture of textiles. It was a pioneer in the use of iron and steel. In 1830 when I was 20, George Stephenson created the first inter city railroad between Manchester and Liverpool. Queen Victoria took the throne when I was 27. By 1850 with just 2 % of the world's population, Britain produced about half the world's manufactured goods. The world's first iron warship was built in England in 1860.

The industrial revolution spread to other countries in Europe besides Britain. It was delayed in France because of the French Revolution and the Napoleonic Wars but eventually caught up to lead to what became known as the "Belle Epoque." It occurred in certain regions of Germany such as the Ruhr and gave rise to the railroads and the great industrial families such as the Krupps and the machine tool manufacturers. Italy came together as a country in what as known as the Risorgimento in the 1860's. In 1869, the Suez Canal opened revolutionizing the carriage of goods by sea.

In the United States, the industrial revolution followed that of Great Britain. Factories, steamships, and railroads all proliferated.

In 1790, Samuel Slater opened the first textile mill in Pawtucket, Rhode Island. In 1793, Eli Whitney invented the cotton gin. Three years before I was born, Robert Fulton opened the first steamboat on the Hudson. The year after I was born, Francis Cabot Lowell carried to America the secret of the British power loom. The Erie Canal was completed in 1825. The Farmington Canal opened in 1828. Cyrus McCormick invented the reaper in 1831. Samuel Morse invented the telegraph in 1844 and sent his first message "What God hath wrought." Texas became a state in 1845. The Mormons settled Utah in 1847. In 1849, a regular steamboat service began between the East Coast and California via Cape Horn. In 1853, Elisha Otis invented a brake for elevators paving the way for the construction of tall buildings. Four years after the Civil War, the first transcontinental railroad was completed. Alaska was purchased from Russia in 1867. The first commercial telephone exchange opened in New Haven in 1878.

The industrialization of America was accompanied by cultural, demographic, and political changes. The wagon trains started leaving for California in 1841. The University of Notre Dame was founded in 1842. Edgar Allen Poe started publishing his writings in the 1840's. Despite opposition from Northern Whigs such as myself, the Mexican War began in 1846. In 1851, the Great Exhibition took place at the Crystal Palace in London and featured many American products. 1851 saw the publication of *Moby Dick* by Herman Melville and *The House of Seven Gables* by Nathaniel Hawthorne. Harriet Beecher Stowe's *Uncle Tom's Cabin* was published in 1852. The Republican Party was founded in Ripon, Wisconsin in 1854. The Supreme Court decided the Dred Scott case in 1857. Lincoln's Gettysburg address was delivered in 1863. The first professional baseball game was played in 1871. The Women's Christian Temperance Union was formed in 1873. As the 1870's passed into the 1890's, the country was entering what came to be called the "Gilded Age."

It was during this time that Deep River came to be

called the "Queen of the Valley": a name based on its prosperity — a prosperity derived primarily from its ivory industry but from other industries as well.

The Industrial Revolution in Deep River saw the numerous sawmills that were powered by the river (The Deep River — not the Connecticut). There was the woodworking tools: the Denisons for the planes and Williams & Marvin for the wood turners. There were the stone quarries. There was the Jennings factory which made the auger bits. There was the Denison shipyard of which I have spoken previously and which prospered until 1869.

The industrial prosperity of Deep River was also accompanied by local social, religious, educational, and cultural changes. Yankee peddlers became a thing of the past with the opening of the Green Store. A Post Office opened in 1827. Billy Winters arrived on the Underground Railroad in the 1820's and showed that a black man could prosper. The new Congregational church was built in 1833. St. Joseph's Catholic Church in Chester was built in 1856. The Deep River Bank opened in 1849. The Wahginnicut House Hotel opened at the end of Kirtland Street in 1854. The Connecticut Valley Railroad opened in July 1871 and started going north from Saybrook to Deep River the following year.

But most of all it was the ivory industry that accounted for Deep River's prosperity. The ivory business was started early in the century by several industrialists such as Ezra Williams, the Pratt Brothers, and Alfred Worthington, and most importantly George Read. But the business became dominant when Pratt, Read, & Company was founded in

1866. When the factory caught fire in 1881, a new one of brick was built. Several ivory products were manufactured including combs, mechanical pencils, and other novelties. But the dominant product was piano keyboards. Pianos became extremely popular by mid-century. A piano became the hallmark of prosperity for middle class families. This gave rise to great demand for ivory products. By mid century, Comstock Cheney in Essex and Pratt Read in Deep River accounted for 90% of the country's ivory business.

Pratt Read was the largest employer in Deep River and provided jobs for many people.

Manufacturing Piano Keyboards

The ivory used in the Deep River factory came from the tusks of African elephants which were carried by hand to the market on the island of Zanzibar off Africa's southeastern coast. George Cheney of Essex spent ten years in Zanzibar as an ivory trader. Ernst D. Moore, a buyer for Pratt Read, did likewise.

E. D. Moore, Ivory Buyer for Pratt Read

Although dimly realized at the time, the process of ivory procurement was cruel and exploitative. Arab slave traders would travel to the African interior, ingratiate themselves with the natives, and gather the tusks. Once they had enough tusks, the Arabs would provoke a fight with the natives, kill some of them, and force the others while chained together to carry the tusks on the long journey to the market town of Zanzibar. Many natives died along the way. Once in Zanzibar, the slaves would be sold in the slave market and the tusks delivered to the Western traders.

Zanzibar Slave Market

The most prominent of the Arab slave traders was the warlord Tippu Tib (formally known as Hamed Bin Muhammed Bin Duma Bin Raja) — a man so powerful that he has been called the "Napoleon" of Africa.

When the wasn't dealing the tusks, Tippu Tib also played a role in the famous explorations of Stanley and Livingston in the African interior. Both Stanley and Livingstone hated the African slave trade but they were forced to live with it.

Tippu Tib

Henry Morton Stanley was one of the great swashbucklers of the Nineteenth Century. Born to poverty in England, he drifted to America where he fought on both sides in the Civil War. He then spent years in Africa searching for the sources of the Nile and Congo rivers and scouting the territory for Leopold, King of the Belgians.

David Livingstone was a Scottish physician and missionary who also explored the African interior. For six years, he was completely cut off from contact with the West. Tippu Tib helped Livingstone survive in the wilderness and aided Stanley in finding Livingstone in the famous meeting of the two in the town of Ujiji near Lake Tanganyika where Stanley is reported to have uttered the famous and proper British greeting (albeit of questionable authenticity) "Dr. Livingstone, I presume."

I remember hearing about the ivory slave trade and the Stanley and Livingstone adventures but I did not pay it much mind. What happened in Zanzibar didn't seem too important in Deep River.

Oceangoing ships would carry the tusks to American ports such as Boston and New York. The cargo would then be ferried by coasting vessels to the Landing in Deep River where they were unloaded and carted up Kirtland Street to the Pratt Read Factory.

At age 55, I had a desire to slow down from the strenuous activity of ocean seagoing. The need for coasting vessels to Deep River created a niche for me. I procured my own sailing schooner. For over a decade I used it to ferry goods back and forth. While we carried many types of freight, the most common exchange was local products to New York and ivory back from New York to the Landing.

Carting Tusks to the Factory

My work as a coaster also allowed me to appreciate the domesticity of Deep River life. I tended a small garden in our back yard. My favorite books were *Alice in Wonderland* by Lewis Carroll and *Twenty Thousand Leagues Under the Sea* by Jules Verne. Although I did not read it, I heard of a new book by Charles Darwin called *The Origin of the Species* which revolutionized man's knowledge of evolution. I was especially interested because much of Darwin's research was based on what he observed in the Galapagos Islands which he reached on the voyage of the ship *Beagle*. My favorite music was the Civil War songs and folk tunes. I continued to read the Connecticut Courant from Hartford and occasionally the Connecticut Constitution from Middletown.

Watching Wings on Water

Chapter 11

SLOWING DOWN

THERE IS A TRADITION OF FORMER DEEP RIVER SEA CAPTAINS retiring to a life of service to the community.

The best example is Joseph Post. After his retirement in 1836, he became a director of the Fountain Hill Cemetery, the president of the Deep River Savings Bank, a founding member of the Hills Academy and the Fire Company in Essex. He established the first lighthouse on the Connecticut River. He served as the Commissioner of Highways for Essex and Deep River and built many bridges and roads. He built a house in Essex which he later sold to a member of the family. He then moved to the Post family homestead at Devil's Wharf in Deep River.

I was never able to match Joseph's accomplishments. But I did my part. I did a little farming. After so many years at sea, I found it comforting to get my hands dirty on the land. I also served on the board of the Deep River Savings Bank. We visited our son Tad and daughter Emma both of whom had moved to the Boston area. Neither of them followed the tradition of the sea. Both of them had children of their own and we enjoyed seeing our grandchildren. Tad had become an accountant and Emma was a part time teacher. I suppose these were good professions for the new century.

I was enjoying my time as a landsman. But I never tired of hearing stories of the sea.

I was especially interested in the stories told by or about the Deep River captains. This was especially true of the two sons of Joe Post: Pritchard Post and David Rowland Post.

Pritchard sailed on many ships (*Devonshire, Peter Hattrick, Orphan*) and was master of brig *Alma* and the steamer *Charles W. Lord*. David also sailed on many ships (*Erastus Brainerd, Emily C. Dickenson, Albion, Francis A. Palmer, James Edwards*) and was master of no less than three clippers, the *Cambrian*, the *Bertreaux* and the *M.E. Watson*. His wife Kate accompanied him on many voyages. He retired in 1889 and became Deep River's Postmaster.

The Bertreaux

The Cambrian

The M.E.Watson

I ALSO ENJOYED the stories of Tapping Spencer, Stillman Tiley, Samuel Shailer, and the Southworths.

But it was not just stories of the past. There were still many Deep River connected mariners sailing the seas. George D. Morrison married Joseph Post's daughter. He commanded the ships *Frank N. Thayer*, *McClellan*, and *Friedlander* on trips to San Francisco, New York, Liverpool, and Calcutta. Morrison Basin in the Straits of Magellan is named for him. Thomas Collins and Albert Pratt were lost at sea.

In the meantime, the world was changing. Construction on the Panama Canal began in 1880. 1884 saw the opening of the Brooklyn Bridge and the publication of *Huckleberry Finn*. The Union School in Deep River was built in 1885. Mary Frances Russell, the widow of Samuel Russell, founded a library in Middletown in 1876 in honor of her husband. And the Statue of Liberty arrived in New York.

Steamboat service was now common on the river. The steamer *City of Hartford* had entered service in 1852 and provided regular service between Hartford and New York for thirty years. It was known for its reliability and the elegance of its interior spaces. But even steam service was not without its perils. On March 29, 1876, the ship crashed into the Air Line Railroad bridge over the river in Middletown causing several injuries to the crew and interruption of both the water and rail service. The ship was repaired and continued service for ten more years (the latter three under the the new name *Capitol City*).

The City of Hartford

My slowing down period coincided with changes at the Landing. The Denison shipyard was now gone. Joseph Smith built his factory on what had been the sail loft and manufactured bright wire goods such as crochet hooks and boot button hooks. Trains went through every day and the whistle could be heard all over town. Soot from the engine covered porches and outdoor furniture. Ivory for the Pratt Read factory was now arriving by train rather than by boat. C.D. Fitch's Salt Warehouse covered most of the original wharf and and was the site of a spectacular fire in June 1881. The colors from the burning salt made quite a display and many residents of Kirtland Street turned out on their porches to watch. The Wahginnicut House presided over the scene like a stately mansion. White sails over the river could be seen every day continuing to inspire men to go to sea.

And I spent time in the village talking with friends about my stories. After a while they got tired of hearing them. That's when I figured that as long as I was telling my stories, I might as well write them down. That is the way by which people in the future can hear and see what it was like to be a seafarer in the Nineteenth Century. These stories are what became this book.

I also decided to make a scrapbook of pictures of some of the most well known houses on Kirtland Street. Here are a few samples. I am continuing this process. I am sorry that I do not have more at this time.

137 Kirtland St.

131 Kirtland St.

115 Kirtland St.

As I stood on my porch gazing over the river and daydreaming, I could not help but think of the Margaret Sangster poem about the Old Sailor.

I've crossed the bar at last mates,
My longest voyage is done;
And I can sit there peaceful.
And watch the setting sun
A smiling kind of glad like
Upon the waves so free,
My longest voyage is done, mates,
But oh, the heart of me,
Is out where sea meets skyline!
My longest voyage is done . . . .
But — can I sit, in peace, mates,
And watch the setting sun?

Wake at Sunset

Chapter 12

Looking Back

During my time in China, I would hear the expression "May you live in Interesting times." As I look back over the wake of my journey, I think that I have lived this expression.

My thoughts turn to the path of my country, the path of my town, the moral dilemmas of history, and the pleasures of small town life.

I was born in the shadow of the birth of a new country. As I grew to maturity, I saw my new country become large, wealthy, and powerful as it took its place among the great nations of the world. I saw a proliferation of inventions that would have been inconceivable only decades before and which made our lives richer and more free. I take great pride in the small role that I have played in this process.

But the path was not always rosy. I saw my country tear itself apart over the Civil War. I don't think I could have done anything to prevent it. But I never wavered in my hatred of slavery in my own country. For this I was willing to fight for five years in the Navy. It seems easy to describe in hindsight but it was hard, fearful, and dangerous at the time.

I have also watched my town go from a small settlement in the wake of the Revolution to the Queen of the Valley. And the course of this process was marked by a great seafaring tradition which is the subject of my story. I have already told the story of the heroics of Samuel W. Mather. And the the epitome of this story is the Post family — Deep River's dynasty of the sea. For generations, the Post family has produced some of the finest mariners the world has ever known. They were active in the Revolution and before. In the early history of their new country, they were active packet captains in the merchant marine service to Europe. Some were active in the Civil War (John E. Rockwell — the son of Olive Post is buried at Arlington). And when the age of sail reached its apogee with the clipper ships, they were active in the exciting races to China. There were many of such individuals. There will never be a way in which I can match the accomplishments of these Deep River Captains. But I at least can tell their story.

My thoughts also turned to a moral ambiguity of history — a form of historical revisionism by which a custom or practice which seems acceptable at one time or place becomes condemned in another. I have experienced this in three circumstances in my own life.

The first was the transport of sugar from the Caribbean plantations. For me, it was simply a matter of picking up a cargo and serving a market in my own country while earning an income and acquiring a skill. Despite my hatred of slavery in our own southern states, I never gave more than a passing thought to the slavery of the sugar plantations.

The second was the plunder of the elephants for the ivory tusks and the native slavery that was required to carry them to Zanzibar. I had heard of this from the then traders. I had even heard that the practice was condemned by Stanley and Livingstone. But I never thought about it as I ferried the tusks from the customs ports to the Landing. Zanzibar was part of what we called the "Darkest Africa"—it was just too far away.

The third was transport of opium to China. I was never fond of opium cargoes. But I never refused them. I gave little thought to the fact that we were helping to make China a nation of drug addicts. For us, it was a matter of rights to free trade and the opportunity to make a fortune in the process. To build a beautiful Greek Revival house and fill it with priceless Oriental furniture (or perhaps a castle in the Hebrides).

Does my conscience bother me about these things? Maybe it does a little now but it never did much at the time. Why was I willing to risk my life fighting against slavery in my own country but relatively indifferent to it in other places? This is a moral question that I can never solve and it causes me ceaseless wonder.

Between my trips at sea, I was able to enjoy the pleasures of a unique New England small town.

I was able to see the richness of other cultures around

the world. This was especially true of China which was one of the world's oldest civilizations.

I was blessed with friends and family.

And I was able to do things that I hope made the world a better place.

I have enjoyed telling you about all this.

I hope you have learned something about my times.

And for all of you whether mariners or not, my wish is for fair winds and a following sea.

Epilogue

The romance of the age of sail was fading as of 1890 — the time we have established for the hypothesized death of our fictitious captain Standish. But whether they be sail or steam, ships were still sailing and Deep River sea captains were still in command. And history marched on.

After 1890

In 1902-1903, George D. Morrison of Deep River was in command of the *Texan* as she sailed for the American Hawaiian Steamship Company between the East and West coasts as well as South America. He was also master of the *Vigilant* when it carried coal to Admiral Dewey's fleet in the Philippines.

Charles Munson was the father of Charles Newton Munson who lived at the Stone House in the early 20th Century. The elder Munson led a life of adventure on the sea. At age 17, he signed on the clipper *M.B. Palmer* bound for China. On his return, he entered the Revenue Service stationed in Key West Florida. He saw service in or near Cuba waters with the Mexican International Steamship Line and the Ward Line and Florida coastal service with the Clyde Line. His Cuban service proved handy in the Spanish American War where he smuggled arms into Cuba on the ship *Three Friends* and was on the *Merrimac* when it was purposely sunk in an effort to block the Spanish fleet in Havana Harbor.

Samuel Shailer and Tapping Spencer were still active after 1890 although not much about them is known.

We have a memorial to the unknown soldier. But not to the unknown sailor. Perhaps we should have one (Selectmen take note!). In some cases, we know the names of our sailors but not their stories. In other cases, we know not their names. But there were undoubtedly many sailors whose adventures rivaled those of our Mr. Standish. Let us give a toast to the unknown sailors from our town who sailed the oceans of the world.

Preservation

Many of these great ships (or replicas) are preserved today. The clipper *Cutty Sark* is preserved in dry dock at Greenwich, England. The *Constitution* ("Old Ironsides") is at the Navy Yard in Boston. The *Eagle* is the Coast Guard's training vessel home ported in New London. The whaler *J.W. Morgan* (and sometimes the *Amistad*) may be found at Mystic Seaport. The *Onrust* (the ship of Adrian Block) belongs to the River Museum in Essex. A model of the *Sea Witch* may be found at the Kennedy Presidential Museum and Library in Boston. Go to see these vessels and imagine what it must have been like to sail them.

Houses

Deep River families still live in houses originally built by these seafarers. Many other local houses are of the Greek Revival style. Hopefully these houses will serve as reminders of the magic of the sea.

Historical Revisionism

The historical revisionism of which Joshua spoke in his *Looking Back* Chapter was felt more keenly in later years.

In the matter of selling opium to the Chinese, Robert B. Forbes and Warren Delano were reportedly of unbothered conscience from these activities. Not so much with the Chinese. Sun Yat-sen, the leader of modern China, was motivated to overthrow the Qing Dynasty by the humiliations it tolerated from the West. He laid stress on independence from imperialist foreign domination. This is a recurrent theme in Chinese policy today.

In the matter of trading in ivory, a dramatic repudiation of his own former activities was revealed in a book called *Ivory, Scourge of Africa* written by Ernst D. Moore in Chester, Connecticut and published by Harper & Brothers in 1931. Moore describes the rapacious attitudes of trade especially of the Arab tribal leader Tippu Tib. Moore does not mince words. His introduction includes the following sentence:

> *I gathered the story of the scourge of Africa, of the ivory treasure that was garnered in the blood of beast and man in a welter of cruelty and carnage that the world never will see again.*

Moore's epigram contains the following poetic words:

> *I, too, have slept in the arms of Zanzibar, have been her slave, and am her lover still. To her, lovely and cruel mistress, I dedicate this volume of her misdeeds*

It is hard to imagine the jarring effect such words would have had in the Queen of the Valley of the Nineteenth Century.

Today, of course, Deep River has confronted its legacy. There is a statue of an elephant outside the Town Hall acknowledging the elephant deaths and the slavery and containing the words *We Honor the Elephant*.

World Trade

The massive container ships of today would have been unimaginable to Joshua's generation. But the history is the same.

The Galleons on the Spanish Main. The Hanseatic League of the Baltic. The Chinese Silk Road. For millennia, men have sought the products of other countries.

The cars of today we bring from Japan are like the horses of yesteryear we brought to the Caribbean. The oil we once burned from the whales is like the oil we now burn from the Saudi's. The crops our farmers traded for sugar in the Caribbean are like the crops our farmers now sell to the world. Amazed as he might have been by the changes, Joshua would have recognized these things.

As we do today, the Americans of Joshua's time debated the merits of the trading of the world. Throughout the latter part of the Nineteenth Century, trade protectionism was high in America and often controversial. The tariff was the major issue during the election campaign of Grover Cleveland in 1892. Is free trade an economic theory that lifts all boats? Do trade wars do more harm than good? Or are tariffs needed to stem the flow of cheap imports or slow the drain of jobs from the rust belt? Joshua would have recognized these debates.

The Meaning of History

Think of what you are doing today. It is probably important to you. Stretch it out for a few weeks — maybe a few months. By the time you get to a year, you are talking about history. Your history is your mark on the continuum of tine.

It is good to be on the right side of history. History may zig and zag like a clipper but it has a certain gravity, an inevitability, a bending of the arc. He who understands his history today will probably make the right choices tomorrow. Joshua would have understood these things.

Most explanations of the meaning of history end as we end here with the famous words attributed to the philosopher George Santayana:

> *Those who do not learn history are doomed to repeat it*

Joshua would have known this as well.

THANK you for reading this book.

I HOPE you have enjoyed it.

Acknowledgments

Much of the credit for this book is due to Rhonda Forristall, the curator of the Deep River Historical Society. Rhonda furnished invaluable help in providing information, wise guidance, and general encouragement.

Rhonda is retired from Middlesex Hospital after a career in critical care and emergency room nursing. She is the author of three books: *Heroes of Deep River* (with her husband) — a book about the Fire Department; *Who Was Daniel Fisher* — a book about William Winters and the Underground Railroad; and *Waterfalls to the Wharf & Beyond* — a book about Deep River during the Industrial Revolution.

Of equal credit is our book designer Dominick Bosco from Chester. Dominick is, himself, a writer and publisher. Without Dominick's skill and perseverance, this and other books of mine would have been impossible.

I would also like to thank Ruth Major who has graciously allowed me to use her painting of the shipyard which appears as the frontispiece for Chapter Seven. Ruth is the co-author of the book entitled *Connecticut River Shipbuilding* and she is a descendant of the legendary Post family.

Last but by no means least, I would like to acknowledge the advice and assistance from the present and former presidents of the Deep River Historical Society: Jerry Roberts, Bruce Edgerton, and Geoff Hostetler.

All mistakes and omissions are mine alone.

About The Images

This book contains 56 images. Many are artwork. They are identified below by number, book page, caption (in Italics), and provenance information. Twelve images are the frontispieces to each chapter. The remainder are contained within the text. Several images are reproduced with permission of the artist or institution as indicated. Many other images are from the files of the Deep River Historical Society. All the rest are taken from the Wikimedia Commons website and are in the public domain via the Creative Commons License.

1) Cover: *The Flying Cloud*
   Clipper *Flying Cloud,* Photo of painting by Jack Spurling. San Francisco History Center, Public Library, and Historical photograph collection. Written on back: Type: clipper ship. Donald McKay, East Boston, 1851.

2) Internal Cover: *The Stone House*
   Home of the Deep River Historical Society
   Reproduced with permission of artist Lori Lenz

3) [p.xv] *Telling Tales of the Sea*
   The Pilots: Painting by Gary Melcher (1887)
   The print is from after page 140 of *Recent Ideals of American Art* published by D. Appleton & Co., c.1888-1890. Melcher's original oil painting is in the collection of the Frye Museum in Seattle. Melcher painted it between 1887-1888. It was exhibited at the Salon in Paris in 1888.

4) [p.6] *The Constitution and the Guerriere*
   Engraved by Thomas Tiebout after painting by Thomas Burch

5) [p.12] *Comings and Goings at the Landing*
   Down East Latch Strings, or Seashore, Lakes, and Mountains by the Boston and Maine Railroad Description of the tourist region of New England (1887). Artist: Ingersol, Ernest (1852-1946). Claire T. Carney Library, University of Massachusetts Dartmouth

6) [p.16] *My son, you should go to the sea*
   Henry Ward Ranger (1858-1916), New England Village. Sale at Christies 3/4/2016

7) [p.20] *South Sea Whaling*
   South Sea Whaling Fisher Ships *Amelia Wilson* and *Castor* off the island of Buru. 1 January 1825. National Library of New Zealand. Color aquatint engraving by T. Sutherland of painting by W.J. Higgins.

8) [p.27] *Aloft in a Gale*
   On board the ship *Garthsnead* at sea. A view from high up in the rigging. State Library of Victoria. Allen C. Green collection of glass negatives. Author: Allen C. Green, George Schutze, or Alexander Turner.

9) [p.29] *Harpooning the Whale*
   Shooting the Harpoon at a Whale — J. Heaviestd Clark (1771-1836). Corel Professional Photos.

10) [p.30] *Yankee Whalers in The Ocean*
    The Whaling ship *Pacific* by William Duke (1848). Gallery of South Australia. M.J.M. Carter AO Collection through the Gallery of South Australia Foundation to mark the Gallery's 125th anniversary.

11) [p.32] *Yale College*
    A View of the Buildings of Yale College of New Haven, 1807. Lithograph published by A. Doolittle

& Sons, New Haven. Courtesy of the Yale Manuscripts and Archives Digital Images Database. Amos Doolittle or workshop.

12) [p.38] *Brig Bound for Barbados*
John Scott, *The Collier Brig Mary*. Signed J. Scott 1855. South Shields Museum and Arts Gallery, UK.

13) [p.40] *Caribbean Sugar Plantation*
Sugar Plantation. Library of Congress Prints and Photographs division.

14) [p.41] *Shipping the Sugar*
Shipping Sugar. From William Clark's Ten Views of the Island of Antigua, 1823. Royal Museums Greenwich Collection. National Maritime Museum, Greenwich, London. Creative Commons License CC-RY-NC- SA-3.0 license.

15) [p. 46] *Cutting the Cane*
The Great South Sugar Plantation, Louisiana, Edward King (Hartford, Conn. 1875), p.83. Special Collections,

16) [p. 48] *The Launch*
Painting by Ruth Major This image is reproduced from an original painting by Ruth Major, an artist from Martha's Vineyard. Ms. Major is the co-author of the recently published book entitled *Connecticut River Shipbuilding*. She has graciously allowed me to use the image for this book. The Deep River

seafarers of the Post family are Ruth's ancestors. The intended subject of the painting is the Essex shipyard launch of the ship *Orphan* for Captain John Urqhuart. I have selected it as an evocative representation of the Connecticut shipyards generally (although the Denison Yard had the capability to launch a ship sideways).

17)[p. 50] *The Denison Shipyard*
   Photograph reproduced from the files of the Deep River Historical Society.

18)[p. 51] *The Oliver Cromwell*
   Image provided courtesy of the Connecticut River Museum

19)[p. 54] *The Amistad*
   Contemporary painting of the vessel *La Amistad* off Culloden Point, Long Island New York on 26 August 1839 on the left of the *U.S.S. Washington* of the U.S. Navy (oil painting). Artist unknown.

20)[p. 56] *Greek Revival House*
   The John P. King House, New London, CT. 13 Prospect St. between Federal Street and Bulkeley Place in New London. Built c. 1840 in Greek Revival style. Part of the Prospect Street Historic District.

21)[p. 62] *The Flying Cloud*
   Clipper *Flying Cloud*, Photo of painting by Jack

Spurling. San Francisco History Center, Public Library, and Historical photograph collection. Written on back: Type: clipper ship. Donald McKay, East Boston, 1851.

22)[p. 66] *Howqua*
Howqua, George Chinnery (1774-1852) Hong Merchant Howqua.

23)[p. 67] *Chinese Opium Den*
Guonouwan opium den c. 1920. Postcard published 1910-1920 showing opium users in an opium den in the French leased territory of Lwang- Tchpou-Wan now Guanzhouwan. Author: Fang-Tang-San.

24)[p. 68] *Qing Emperor Amijmur*
"Daeguang Emperor Court Dress, 18th-19th Century. Palace Museum Beijing.

25)[p.69] *A Scene from the Opium Wars*
The 98th Regiment of Foot at the Attack on Chin-King-Foo, 21 July 1842. Richard Simkin (1840-1928). S.K. Brown Military Collection, Brown University Library Digital Repository.

26)[p. 70] *The Samuel Russell House*
Wesleyan University Photograph by Jon Mabel.

27)[p. 72] *The Sea Witch*
US clipper *Sea Witch* built by John W. Griffiths

(1809- 1882). Unknown Chinese Artist of the Mid-19th Century.

28)[p. 75] *Sailing Card*
Sailing card for the clipper ship *California*, G.F. Nesbitt & Co., printer. Derivative work: Jim Evans.

29)[p.76] *San Francisco 1849*
Title: San Francisco, Author: Popular Graphic Arts. Library of Congress prints and photographs division.

30)[p. 77] *The Niantic Hotel, San Francisco*
An 1855 lithograph of ships being used as businesses in San Francisco, Apollo storeship and Niantic Hotel. Unknown artist. U.C. Berkeley Bancroft Library.

31)[p. 80] *The Robert Center*
Reproduced from the original painting at the Deep River Historical Society.

32)[p. 81] *Samuel W. Mather*
Reproduced from a photograph in the files of the Deep River Historical Society.

33)[p. 82] *The Nightingale*
Nightingale (ship 1851). From the book: *The Clipper Ship Era: an epitome of famous American and British ships, their owners, commanders, and crews*

1843-1869. Author: Clark, Arthur Hamilton (1841-1922). New York, G.P. Putnam's Sons (1910). Contributor: University of California Libraries.

34)[p. 85] *The Lord of the Isles*
1853 clipper ship. From Lubbock, Basil, *The China Clippers* (4th ed.), Glasgow, James Brown & Son. P. 127.

35)[p. 88] *Hong Kong, 1850*
Hong Kong Harbor 1850. Vallejo Gallery. Anonymous artist.

36)[p. 90] *Ariel and Taeping*
The clipper *Ariel* and *Taeping* racing home with the new season tea. Montague Dawson (1890-1973)

37)[p. 92] The *Kearsarge* and the *Alabama* (Manet)
Edouard Manet, French — The Battle of the *U.S.S. Kearsarge* and the *C.S.S. Alabama* Google Art Project. Philadelphia Museum of Art.

38)[p. 95] *The Sinking of the Petrel*
"Destruction of the privateer *Petrel* by the *St. Lawrence*". From the *Great Civil War*, Vol I by Robert Townes, M.D. and Benjamin G. Smith, published by Virtue and Yorston 1865. Missouri History Museum.

39)[p. 96] *The Monitor and the Merrimac*
Terrific Combat between Monitor, 2 guns and

Merrimac, 10 guns, The first fight between iron clad ships of war in Hampton Roads, March 9, 1862. Currier & Ives. Library of Congress.

40)[p. 98] *The Battle of Cherbourg*
   USS Kearsarge v. CSS Alabama by Antonio Jacobson (1850-1921), 1914. Source: Vallejo.

41)[p. 100] *A Coasting Schooner*
   Schooner. National Gallery of Art. Gift of Lucy Galpin Moorhead in memory of William S. Moorhead and the Honorable William S. Moorhead, Jr. and in honor of the 50th anniversary of the National Gallery of Art.

42)[p. 102] The Vail under Construction with the Wahginnicut Hotel in the Foreground and Eustacia Island in the Background.
   Reproduced from the files of the Deep River Historical Society.

43)[p. 106] *Manufacturing Piano Keyboards*
   Reproduced from the files of the Deep River Historical Society.

44)[p. 107] *Ernst D. Moore, Ivory Buyer for Pratt Read*
   Reproduced from the files of the Deep River Historical Society

45)[p. 108] *Zanzibar Slave Market*
   Un marche aux esclaves a Zanzibar, per Emile Bayard (1837-1891). Source: historique de vielle. Author: Henri Theophile Hildibrand (1894-1897).

46)[p. 109] *Tippu Tib*
   Painting in House of Wonders Museum, Stone Town, Zanzibar.

47)[p. 111] *Carting Tusks to the Factory*
   Reproduced from the files of the Deep River Historical Society.

48)[p. 112] *Watching Wings on Water*
   Scribner's magazine (1887). Library — Robarts - University of Toronto, Publisher: New York, C. Scribner's Sons.Internet Archive Book Images.

49)[p. 114] *The Bertreaux*
   Reproduced from the original painting at the Stone House.

50)[p. 115] *The Cambrian*
   Reproduced from the original painting at the Stone House.

51)[p.115] *M.E. Watson*
   Reproduced from the files of the Deep River Historical Society.

52)[p. 117] *The City of Hartford*
    City of Hartford (1852 steamboat). Unknown author. Source: Jacobus Melancthon (1958), The Connecticut River Steamboat Story, Hartford, CT, The Connecticut Historical Society.

53)[p. 118] *137 Kirtland St.*
    Reproduced from the files of the Deep River Historical Society.

54)[p. 119] *131 Kirtland St.*
    Reproduced from the files of the Deep River Historical Society.

55)[p. 119] *115 Kirtland St.*
    Reproduced from the files of the Deep River Historical Society.

56)[p. 122] *Wake at Sunset*
    Wake in the Sunset. Vince Alongi from Delta, B.C., Canada.

Index

A

Aberdeen 86
Admiral Keppel 51
Admiral Goldsborough 95
Admiral Samuel Phillips Lee 95
Africa 4, 46, 53, 108, 109, 125, 129, 130
Alabama 4, 92, 97, 98, 142, 143
Alaska 104
Albion 114
Alfred Lord Tennyson 23
Alma 114
Almira 27
Alsop and Company 42, 43, 44
American Hawaiian Steamship Company 127
Amistad 53, 54, 128, 139
Anaconda Plan 94
Andrew, Henry 97
Angier Point 64, 83
Ariel 89, 90, 142
Arnold, Hanson 57, 79
Arnold, Joseph 57, 79
Arnold, Justus, 57, 79
Australia 3, 29, 64, 82, 83, 84, 85, 137, 137
Azores 25, 25

B

Barbados 24, 38, 40, 42, 43, 44, 45, 138
Barbary Pirates 9
Battle of Bunker Hill 7
Battle of Cherbourg 98, 99, 143
Battle of Hampton Roads 3
Battle of New Orleans 8
Battle of Waterloo 8
Beagle Channel 26, 111
Belgravia 45
Belle Epoque 103
Bengal 67
Bertreaux 114, 144
Bidwell, Edwin 57
Block, Adrian 128

Brainerd, Erastus 114
Brouwer Route 78
Byron, Lord 35

C

C. D. Fitch Salt Warehouse 117
California Gold Rush 3, 64, 83
Cambrian 114, 115, 144
Canton 65, 66, 67, 73, 84, 86
Cape Fear 95
Cape Horn 1, 24, 26, 65, 73, 74, 104
Cape of Good Hope 64
Caribbean Sugar Trade 2, 39, 40, 41, 42, 43, 45, 125, 131
Carroll, Lewis 111
Causeway Bay 86
Challenger 3, 82, 83
Chase 30
Cherbourg, France 4
Chester 81, 105, 129, 133
Chile 27, 28, 74

China 3, 16, 64, 65, 66, 67, 69, 70, 71, 72, 73, 75, 82, 83, 84, 85, 86, 88, 89, 90, 123, 124, 125, 126, 128, 129, 142
Chinoiserie 65
Civil War 3, 84, 93, 97, 99, 101, 102, 104, 109, 111, 123, 124, 142
Cleveland, Grover 131
Clipper Route 64, 73, 78, 85
Coleridge, Samuel Taylor 35
Collins, Thomas Massie 80
Congregational Church 14, 34, 54, 105
Connecticut Courant 9, 15, 111
Connecticut Valley Railroad 105
Cooper, James Fennimore 15, 35, 66, 87
Coquimbo, Chile 28
Coral Sea 29
Crandall, Prudence 46
Crawford, Ninian 87

Crimean War 87

Cromwell, Oliver 50, 51, 139

Cutty Sark 64, 90, 128

D

Darwin, Charles 111

Day, Jeremiah 34

Decatur, Steven 9

Declaration of Independence 9

Deep River 1, 2, 3, 4, 7, 13, 24, 31, 36, 42, 43, 47, 49, 51, 53, 57, 60, 77, 79, 80, 81, 83, 97, 104, 105, 106, 110, 111, 113, 114, 116, 124, 127, 129, 130, 133, 134, 135 136, 139, 141, 143, 144, 145

Deep River Savings Bank 113

Delano, Warren 73, 129

Denison Shipyard 50, 105, 117, 139

Denison, Thomas 2, 49, 52

Devonshire 114

Dickens, Charles 59

Dickenson, Emily C. 114

Diligent 41

Drake's Passage 26, 27

Dred Scott Case 104

Duke of Wellington 68

Dwight, Timothy 34

E

Edwards, James 114

Embargo of 1807 8

Emirs 30

Emmagene, Eudora 81

Epaphroditas Bailey

Era of Good Feeling 13

Erie Canal 103

Essex 2, 8, 17, 41, 49, 50, 51, 57, 106, 107, 113, 129, 136, 139,

F

Farmington Canal 103

Federalist Party 7

Financial Panic of 1837 53

Flemish Horse 27

Flying Cloud 62, 64, 136, 140

Foochow, China 86
Forbes, Robert B. 82, 129
Forrest 53
Fort Sumpter 3, 93
Fountain Hill Cemetery 81, 97, 113
Fulton, Robert 103

G
Galapagos Islands 111
Garrison, William 46
Geneva, Switzerland 98, 99
Gettysburg Address 104
Gilbert Island Group 29
Gilded Age 104
Great Exposition at the Crystal Palace 104
Greek Revival Architecture 104
Green Store 17, 55, 105
Griffiths, John W. 71, 141
Guerriere, HMS 6, 8, 136

H
Haddam 57, 81
Halifax 85

Harrison, Benjamin 58,
Harvard College 35
Havana Harbor 128
Hebrides 73, 125
HMS Boreas 44
Hong Kong 66, 69, 71, 72, 74, 75, 76, 84, 86, 87, 88, 142
Hooker, Thomas 7
Howland & Aspinwall 65, 71, 75

I
Indian Ocean 64
Industrial Revolution 101, 102, 103, 105, 133
Irving, Washington 15

J
Jackson, Andrew 8
Jardine, Andrew 73
Jardine, David 86
Jardine, William 69, 73
Jefferson, Thomas 35

K

Kennedy Library 129

Kingsley, James L. 34

Kirtland Street 1, 2, 9, 14, 16, 36, 49, 55, 57, 81, 105, 110, 117, 118

Kow-Tow 67

Kowloon 86

L

Lake Tanganyika 110

Lane, Thomas Ash 87

Lewis, Island of 73

Lincoln, Abraham 93

Lind, Jenny (The Swedish Nightingale) 82

Liverpool 85, 97, 103, 116, 135

Livingston, David 106, 110, 125

London 3, 10, 16, 21, 30, 45, 53, 58, 64, 69, 82, 83, 84, 86, 86, 89, 104, 128, 138, 139

London Society of West India Planters 45, 139

Longfellow, Henry Wadsworth 58

Loper, James 22

Lord of the Isles 3, 85, 93, 142

Lord Palmerston 69

Lord, Charles W. 114

Lowell, Francis Cabot 103

M

M.B. Palmer (ship) 128

M.E. Watson (ship) 135, 144

Madison, James 9

Manet, Edouard 92, 142

Martha's Vineyard 31, 138

Mather, Frank 161

Mather, Samuel W. 81, 124, 141

Mathesen, James 66, 73

Mathesen, Jardine 65

Maury 3, 86

Mayfair 45

McCormick, Cyrus 103

McKay, Donald 59, 63, 136, 140

Melbourne, Australia 84

Melville, Herman 104
Mende 53
Merrimac 3, 96, 128, 142
Mexican War 75, 104
Middletown, Connecticut 65
Monitor 3, 96, 142, 143
Monroe Doctrine 17
Moore, Ernst D. 107, 129, 143
Morrison Basin 116
Morrison, George 116, 127
Morse, Samuel 103
Mosquito Inlet 97
Munson, Charles 127
Mystic 128

N

Nanking 65, 69
Nantucket 1, 21, 22, 23, 28, 30, 31, 33, 34, 35
Nantucket sleigh ride 28
Napoleonic Wars 8, 103
Nelson, Horatio 44
Nelson, Lord Horatio 8, 44

Nevis 44, 45, 45
New Georgia Islands 29
New London 16, 21, 30, 53, 58, 64, 128, 139
New Zealand 30, 137
Niantic Hotel 76, 77, 141
Nicaragua 74
Nightingale 3, 82, 83, 97, 141
Nisbet, Fannie 44

O

Onrust 128
Opium Wars 65, 66, 67, 68, 69, 72, 73, 125, 129, 140
Orphan 114, 139
Otis, Elisha 104

P

Pacific 1, 17, 22, 24, 25, 29, 30, 30, 65, 95, 137
Palmer, Francis A. 114
Palmer, Ned 22
Palmerston, Lord 69
Panama Canal 116
Papua New Guinea 29

Parliament 47, 66, 68, 73

Pearl River 86

Peter Hettrick 114

Petrel 95, 142

Phoebe 30

Plough Bay 30

Poe, Edgar Allen 59, 104

Pompino 53

Post, David Rowland 114, 135

Post, Nathan 7

Potomac River 95

Pratt Brothers 4, 57, 105

Pratt, Jedediah 7

Pratt, Read & Co. 105

Pritchard Post 114

Provision State 41

Putnam, Israel 7

Q

Qing Dynasty 67, 129, 140

Queen of the Valley 4, 101, 105, 124, 130

Queen Victoria 103

R

Ralph Waldo Emerson 59

Read, George 4, 10, 57, 105

Republican Party 104

Repulse Bay 86

Restoration, HMS 51

Risorgimento 103

Robert Center 79, 80, 141

Rogers, Calvin 57

Royal Navy 8, 47, 51, 69, 87

Rufus Baker 57

Russell & Co. 65

Russell, Samuel 65, 70, 116, 140

S

Sampson and Tappan 82

San Francisco 3, 74, 75, 76, 77, 116, 136, 140, 141

Sangster, Margaret 119

Santayana, George 132

Sara 27

Saunders, John N. 80
Saybrook Colony 7
Scotland 73, 85
Scott, Walter 15, 35
Scott, Winfield 94
Sea Witch 3, 71, 72, 73, 75, 83, 129, 141
Shailer, Samuel 116, 128
Shanghai 3, 82, 83, 84
Shelly, Percy Byssche 35
Silliman, Benjamin 34, 58, 142
Slater, Samuel 103
Sophia 30
South & Dimon Yard 71
Southworth Shipyard 2, 49, 51, 52, 57, 58, 116
Southworth, Eli 2, 49, 52, 116
Southworth, Job 51, 52
Spanish American War 128
Spencer, Rev. Orson 14
Splendid 2, 52, 80
St. Deny's 2, 53
St. Lawrence (ship) 3, 95, 142

Standish, Myles 7
Stanley, Henry Morton 109
Statue of Liberty 116
Stephenson, George 103
Stone House 57, 80, 127, 135, 136, 144
Stonington 17
Stornoway 73
Stowe, Harriet Beecher 93, 104
Straits of Magellan 26, 116
Suez Canal 90, 103
Sun Yat-Sen 129
Superior 25, 97, 98
Swift 30

T

Tai Pan 162
Taiping 90
Tapping Spencer 116, 128
Texan 127
The Liberator 46
Thermopylae 64, 90
Three Friends 128
Ticknor, George 35

Tierra del Fuego 26
Tippecanoe and Tyler Too 58
Tippu Tib 108, 109, 110, 129, 144
Trafalgar 8
Transcontinental Railroad 104
Treaty of Washington 98
Trinidad 26
Turkey 67
Tyler, John 58

U

Underground Railroad 105, 133

University of Notre Dame 104
University of Virginia 35, 138
USS Constitution 6, 8, 9, 128, 136
USS Kearsarge 4, 143

V

Vail 102, 102, 143

Valparaiso, Chile 74, 74
Van Buren, Martin 58
Vigilant 127
Virginia 3, 35, 96, 138

W

Wahginnicut House Hotel 102, 117, 143
War of 1812 8, 13, 14, 41
Washington, George 41
Waterman, Bully Bob 72, 74
Watkinson Family 43, 44
Webster, Noah 10
Welles, Gideon 97
Wellington, Duke of 68
Whitney, Eli 103, 103
Whompoa Reach 73, 84
Wilberforce, William 47
Williams, Calvin 57, 80
Williams, Richard Calvin 57, 80
Winters, Billy 105
Wolcott, Oliver, Jr. 9
Women's Christian Temperance Union 104
Wyes, Johan David 15

Y

Yale College 2, 32, 33, 34, 35, 36, 39, 73, 138,

Yale, Elihu 34

Z

Zanzibar 107, 108, 110, 125, 130, 143, 144

Bibliography

A Clipper Ship and Her Commander, Frank J. Mather, Article in the Atlantic Magazine, November 1904

Along the Waterfront at Deep River on the Connecticut — A Brief Maritime History of Our Town in Sailing Ship Days, by Thomas A. Stevens

Connecticut River Master Mariners, by Thomas A. Stevens

Connecticut River Shipbuilding, Wick Griswold and Ruth Major

Deep River, The Illustrated Story of a Connecticut River Town, Daniel J. Connors

Heart of Darkness, Joseph Conrad

Ivory, Scourge of Africa, Ernst D. Moore [Internet Archive]

Moby Dick, Herman Melville

Night Boat to New York, Erik Hesselberg

Two Years Before the Mast, Richard Henry Dana

Uncle Tom's Cabin, Harriett Beecher Stowe

Sea Life in Nelson's Time, John Masefield (1905)[Internet Archive]

The Sea Witch: A Narrative of the Experiences of Capt. Roger Murray and Others in an American Clipper Ship During the Years 1846 to 1856, Alexander Laing

The Wager, David Grann

Tai Pan, James Clavell

The Wine Dark Sea, Patrick O'Brian

Waterfalls to the Wharf & Beyond: Deep River's Role in the Industrial Revolution, Rhonda Forristall

Who Was Daniel Fisher, Rhonda Forristall

Also by Frank Hanley Santoro

Deep River Stories

When Will They Come For Me

More Deep River Stories

The Diary of Valerian Petrovsky

Stories From My Life

The Legend of the White Cowl

About the Author

Frank Hanley Santoro is a resident of Deep River, Connecticut. He is a trustee of the Deep River Historical Society. A graduate of Georgetown and the University of London, he is a retired lawyer and a former Assistant United States Attorney and Army Officer. His retirement avocation is writing. This is his seventh book.